NEW DIRECTIONS FOR COMMUNITY COLLEGES

Arthur M. Cohen
EDITOR-IN-CHIEF

Florence B. Brawer
ASSOCIATE EDITOR

Presidents and Trustees in Partnership: New Roles and Leadership Challenges

Iris M. Weisman
North Carolina State University

George B. Vaughan
North Carolina State University

EDITORS

Number 98, Summer 1997

WITHDRAWN

JOSSEY-BASS PUBLISHERS
San Francisco

ERIC®

Clearinghouse for Community Colleges

PRESIDENTS AND TRUSTEES IN PARTNERSHIP: NEW ROLES AND LEADERSHIP
CHALLENGES
Iris M. Weisman, George B. Vaughan (eds.)
New Directions for Community Colleges, no. 98
Volume XXV, number 2
Arthur M. Cohen, Editor-in-Chief
Florence B. Brawer, Associate Editor

New Directions for Community Colleges is indexed in Current Index to
Journals in Education (ERIC).

Microfilm copies of issues and articles are available in 16mm and 35mm,
as well as microfiche in 105mm, through University Microfilms Inc.,
300 North Zeeb Road, Ann Arbor, Michigan 48106-1346.

ISSN 0194-3081   ISBN 0-7879-9818-4

NEW DIRECTIONS FOR COMMUNITY COLLEGES is part of The Jossey-Bass
Higher and Adult Education Series and is published quarterly by Jossey-
Bass Inc., Publishers, 350 Sansome Street, San Francisco, California
94104-1342, in association with the ERIC Clearinghouse for Community
Colleges. Periodicals postage paid at San Francisco, California, and at
additional mailing offices. POSTMASTER: Send address changes to New
Directions for Community Colleges, Jossey-Bass Inc., Publishers, 350
Sansome Street, San Francisco, California 94104-1342.

SUBSCRIPTIONS cost $55.00 for individuals and $98.00 for institutions,
agencies, and libraries. Prices subject to change.

THE MATERIAL in this publication is based on work sponsored wholly or
in part by the Office of Educational Research and Improvement, U.S.
Department of Education, under contract number RI-93-00-2003. Its contents do not necessarily reflect the views of the Department or any other
agency of the U.S. Government.

EDITORIAL CORRESPONDENCE should be sent to the Editor-in-Chief, Arthur
M. Cohen, at the ERIC Clearinghouse for Community Colleges, Univer-
sity of California, 3051 Moore Hall, 405 Hilgard Avenue, Los Angeles,
California 90024-1521.

Cover photograph © Rene Sheret, After Image, Los Angeles, California, 1990.

Jossey-Bass Web address: http://www.josseybass.com

TCF Manufactured in the United States of America on Lyons Falls Turin
Book. This paper is acid-free and 100 percent totally chlorine-free.

Contents

EDITORS' NOTES

Much has been written about the roles of the president and governing board in leading and managing the nation's community colleges. Rarely, however, have the roles been discussed in one volume, thereby permitting the reader to understand and appreciate the relationship between members of the governing board and the president—a relationship not always free from conflict, but one that must function effectively if the community college is to achieve its potential. This relationship depends upon the honing and use of personal and professional skills by both presidents and trustees to develop a clear understanding of their roles and expectations. Whereas the board-president relationship is important to the progress and achievement of a community college under normal circumstances, an effective relationship is even more critical in times of crisis and change. This volume explores the professional needs, challenges, and roles of community college governing board members and their presidents—and how these factors influence the board-president team.

The volume begins with a presentation of current demographic profiles of trustees and presidents, obtained from a national survey of trustees conducted in 1995 and a national survey of presidents conducted in 1996. The data on trustees and presidents provide a starting point for discussion about the implications of the similarities and differences between community college presidents and trustees. Questions raised in Chapter One help frame the context of the subsequent chapters in the volume.

Chapters Two and Three address the professional and personal development needs of presidents and trustees. In Chapter Two, David R. Pierce and Robert P. Pedersen identify three critical personal characteristics for successful presidents: personal adaptability, role flexibility, and sound judgment. Pierce and Pedersen argue that these qualities are prerequisites for successfully meeting the challenges of the community college presidency, both now and in the future.

In Chapter Three, Gary Davis provides a comprehensive examination of the major components of trustee orientation and professional development programs. The current status of trustee development is discussed, along with methods for motivating trustees to participate in professional development programs. Emphasis is placed on both the personal and the professional aspects of trustee development.

Chapter Four reflects the wisdom and experiences of a community college president and a board chair who have developed and nurtured a successful board-president relationship. Norm Nielsen and Wayne Newton discuss many aspects of establishing and maintaining trust between a governing board and its president. These leaders present their recommendations for using quality leadership, team building, and planning and organization to enhance the board-president relationship.

Community colleges are no exception to the truism that the only constant is change. For community college presidents and trustees, in particular, the ability to respond successfully to change is essential. In Chapter Five, George R. Boggs and Cindra J. Smith present the findings of a study they conducted of eighteen current or former presidents or chancellors regarding the issues surrounding the causes and ramifications of changes in governing board membership. Presidents whose boards have undergone a change in membership are presented with more challenges than merely becoming acquainted with and orienting a new board member; every new seating on the board represents a potential clash of culture, interests, philosophy, and perspective both among trustees and between trustees and presidents. Rounding out the chapter are responses by presidents to board membership changes and strategies that presidents can employ successfully to manage these changes.

Community college boards must also deal with change. Chapter Six explores the role and responsibilities of the board in making smooth transitions in times of change. Montez C. Martin, Jr., translates his experiences as a community college trustee into lessons learned about successfully responding to change. The key to this success is a governing board that has evolved into a cohesive, effective team.

Also familiar to community college presidents and trustees is the notion of crisis. All community colleges face crises; yet some colleges are more successful than others in effectively resolving crisis situations. In Chapter Seven, Sean A. Fanelli analyzes the role of the community college president in handling crises, using examples from his experience as a community college president. "To ensure that a crisis does not become a disaster," he asserts, "three things must be done: communicate, communicate, and communicate." Various kinds of crises that community college presidents face, the strategies for resolving crises, and even the potential benefits of crises are described from the presidential perspective.

Successful resolution of a crisis is a shared responsibility between the president and the board. Phyllis Gutierrez Kenney provides the trustee's perspective on handling crises in Chapter Eight. She states that the board and president can diminish the harmful effects of a crisis through development and implementation of a crisis management plan and presents the necessary components of such a plan. In addition, the importance of an effective board-president relationship in crisis management is discussed.

Chapter Nine focuses on the challenges that community college governing boards and presidents will face in the next millennium. Fred Gaskin examines the evolution of the community college system of governance and the impact of these changes on the role and responsibilities of presidents and boards. Gaskin suggests that presidents and trustees must develop a mutually supportive relationship in order to meet the challenges of the next century. Working together as a team, trustees and presidents can make significant contributions to their community colleges in the areas of access, funding, and political and civic relationships.

The volume concludes with an annotated bibliography of sources and information regarding leadership issues in the community college and the roles and responsibilities of community college trustees and presidents and characteristics of effective board-president relations.

The textbook definition of the difference in roles between trustee and president is that the former makes policy and the latter carries out policy. We believe that there is much more to the board-president relationship. Effective leadership by community college presidents and trustees requires mutual trust, mutual support, and mutual respect. The contributors to this volume underscore how important an effective board-president relationship is to the welfare and well-being of our community colleges, our communities, and our nation.

Iris M. Weisman
George B. Vaughan
Editors

IRIS M. WEISMAN is a research and teaching associate with ACCLAIM at North Carolina State University in Raleigh and the former director of curriculum services for Pima Community College in Tucson.

GEORGE B. VAUGHAN is a professor of higher education at North Carolina State University in Raleigh. Prior to becoming a professor, he served as a community college president for seventeen years.

The majority of community college trustees and presidents have much in common when one considers race or ethnicity, gender, and educational level. Selected characteristics of community college presidents and trustees provide the background for questions and discussion regarding what these characteristics might mean for the board-president team.

Selected Characteristics of Community College Trustees and Presidents

George B. Vaughan, Iris M. Weisman

The authors of this chapter have recently conducted and analyzed the results of national surveys of trustees and presidents of the nation's public community colleges. The primary purpose of this chapter is to present selected information from the surveys in order to describe the individuals who occupy these important positions. One question the authors seek to answer is whether the profiles of trustees and presidents are similar in gender, ethnicity, age, political party preference, and educational level. That is, to what extent are presidents and trustees alike? What are the implications for the community college, especially in terms of leadership diversity? The readers, we hope, are able to draw some conclusions regarding their own institutions from the data on presidents and trustees. Just as importantly, the data may well raise a number of questions, some of which may make trustees and presidents a bit uncomfortable. In any event, we hope that presidents, trustees, and others associated with the community college use the material presented in this chapter and throughout this volume to evaluate the context within which their leaders function and to use this information to improve leadership effectiveness at their institutions.

A second purpose of this chapter is to provide information that may be helpful in understanding and perhaps appreciating more fully the remaining chapters in this volume. For example, it may help if one knows such things as the educational level of trustees before reading about what constitutes a good educational program for them. Similarly, if one understands the level of stress under which presidents function, one may understand more fully why presidents act or react in certain ways when crises occur.

A third purpose of this chapter is to offer our observations and to ask questions based upon the data presented on presidents and trustees. Some but

NEW DIRECTIONS FOR COMMUNITY COLLEGES, no. 98, Summer 1997 © Jossey-Bass Publishers not all of the observations and questions relate to information presented in the other chapters of this volume.

The Surveys

The authors believe that the surveys of trustees and presidents are the first ones ever conducted essentially at the same time. (The trustees' survey was completed in August 1995, and the presidents' survey was completed in August 1996 by the same researchers, thereby providing the opportunity for uniform examination of selected characteristics of trustees and presidents at almost the same point in time.)

The Trustees' Survey. The population for this study was board chairs and trustees of public community college governing boards whose institutions belong to the Association of Community College Trustees (ACCT). Student trustees and ex-officio board members were excluded from the population. Two separate surveys were sent: one to board chairs and one to nonchair trustees of ACCT's member institutions. Six hundred eighteen trustees (171 chairs and 447 nonchairs) returned the survey, a 39 percent response rate. These 618 respondents represent approximately 14 percent of the trustee population.

The Presidents' Survey. The population for this study was presidents of public community colleges whose institutions belong to the American Association of Community Colleges (AACC). Six hundred eighty presidents, approximately 74 percent of the population, responded to the survey.

A Brief Profile

The following information provides some insight into who currently serves as trustees and presidents of the nation's community colleges. We offer observations and questions following each category described. While our questions and observations may help to set the stage for the remainder of the volume, we also hope that the data permit trustees, presidents, and others interested in the community college to use this information to draw conclusions about their institutions. The data reflect a national profile of community college trustees and presidents; the reader is asked to keep in mind that just as all community colleges are different, so are the individuals who serve on their governing boards and who serve as presidents of these institutions. Moreover, no attempt is made in the following discussion to distinguish between elected and appointed governing boards, although some of the observations and questions may be more appropriate to one board selection process than to the other.

Race, Ethnicity, and Gender

Race or ethnicity of trustees. Caucasians dominate the ranks of community college trustees, with 86.6 percent so classifying themselves. The remainder of the trustees fall into the following categories: African American, 7.9 percent;

Hispanic, 2.3 percent; "other," 1.2 percent; Asian American, 1.1 percent; and American Indian, 0.8 percent.

Race or ethnicity of presidents. As is true with trustees, the great majority of community college presidents are Caucasian, with 85.6 percent classifying themselves as such. The remainder of the presidents fall into the following categories: African American, 5.2 percent; Hispanic, 4.9 percent; American Indian, 1.9 percent; Asian American, 1.5 percent; and "other," 0.9 percent. The number of presidents who classify themselves as Caucasian declined from 89 percent in 1991 (Vaughan, Mellander, and Blois, 1994). Both African Americans and Hispanics made modest gains: in 1991, 4.5 percent of the presidents were African American and 3 percent were Hispanic (Vaughan, Mellander, and Blois, 1994).

Gender of trustees. Approximately two-thirds of the trustees are men. The rise in the proportion of female trustees to one in three has been slow but steady over the past decade. Nearly 29 percent of the trustees in 1987 were women (Whitmore, 1987).

Gender of presidents. Approximately 82 percent of the current community college presidents are men. The proportion of female presidents, at 18 percent, has risen approximately 7 percentage points over the last five-year period (Vaughan, Mellander, and Blois, 1994).

Observations and questions. In reading about the gender and race or ethnicity of trustees and presidents, one quickly notes the dominance of white males in the ranks of both presidents and trustees. Although the percentage of female trustees has increased over the years, the percentage of minority trustees remains woefully small. Similarly, the 7 percentage point increase in female presidents since 1991 is encouraging to those who wish to see more women community college presidents but falls far short of bringing about equal representation between the sexes.

The increases diversify the board and the presidency somewhat, but they still leave a white male clearly in charge of the board room and the president's office at most community colleges. Yet, concurrent with an increase in the percentage of female trustees is an increase in the percentage of female presidents.

These observations lead one to ask whether the gender, race, or ethnicity of trustees has any bearing on presidential selection. Is it naïve to assume that the large percentage of white male trustees has had little bearing on the limited selection of minority presidents? Bluntly stated, is the predominantly white "old boys' club" alive and well among trustees and presidents, leaving women and minorities on the periphery of the presidential selection process? Or should boards be applauded for making some progress in bringing more women and minorities into the presidency? Should the board care what the gender or race of the president is as long as he or she performs adequately? Or do governing boards have an obligation to diversify the presidential selection process, providing female and minority role models and mentors for other women and minorities aspiring to the presidency?

Certainly the old argument that there are not any qualified women to fill presidential vacancies is outdated and invalid. Graduate classes in higher education are filled with women; women also occupy many positions such as division chair at the community college level. The empty-pipeline argument has more validity with minorities than with women. What can be done to interest more minorities in community college administration, thus preparing them to become presidents? Furthermore, what can be done to make the pipeline bias-free in relation to gender and race or ethnicity? How these questions are answered and the corresponding actions of presidents and boards may well have a bearing on who leads the community colleges in the first decade of the twenty-first century.

Age

Age of trustees. The youngest trustee responding to the survey was twenty-two; the two oldest were eighty-four. The average age of all trustees is 57.6 years. Approximately 31 percent of the trustees are between fifty and fifty-nine. Approximately 24 percent of the trustees are under fifty, and 45 percent are older than sixty. The average age of trustees has increased from approximately fifty-four in 1987 (Whitmore, 1987).

Age of presidents. The youngest president responding to the survey was twenty-nine; the oldest was seventy-two. The average age of current presidents is 54.3. Over 62 percent of the current presidents are between fifty and fifty-nine. Approximately 20 percent are under fifty, and approximately 17 percent are over sixty. The average age of current presidents has increased from 52.4 in 1991 (Vaughan, Mellander, and Blois, 1994).

Observations and questions. Similar questions to those about race or ethnicity arise when discussing diversity of age on boards. Assertions in the literature suggest that a governing board composed of members of varying ages is preferable to one with all board members close in age (Houle, 1989), or that a mandatory retirement age for trustees is necessary to keep a board vital and effective (Nason, 1982). The data on trustees indicate that although there is a wide range of ages among trustees, the majority (61 percent) are between fifty and sixty-nine. In addition, with nearly 15 percent of the trustees seventy or older, it is clear that a mandatory retirement age for trustees has not been put into effect.

To what extent does a trustee's age affect his or her perceptions? Age, of course, may be related to the breadth of one's life experiences and to one's perceptions and values. On the other hand, people may have a chronological age that seems inconsistent with their intellectual or emotional age; maturity measured in years may not be a good predictor of one's perceptions, values, or ability to function effectively as a trustee.

The fact is, however, that people do age, retire, and leave vacancies on the board and in the presidency. The process of filling presidential and board vacancies raises a number of questions, the most pressing perhaps being whether trustees should work to diversify governing boards and the presidency in terms of increasing the number of women and minority trustees and presidents. Retirements present an *ever-present* opportunity to appoint women and minorities to the governing boards and to the presidency. While trustees rarely have the legal authority to appoint someone to the governing board, they are often influential with those individuals and agencies that do appoint trustees. Should they use this influence to have more women and minorities appointed to the governing board?

Another question in relation to presidential vacancies—one that is often not asked—is what role current presidents play in selecting future presidents. (This question is also relevant to the discussion of gender and minority status of presidents and trustees.) Certainly through mentoring and selecting top-level administrators such as vice presidents and deans, presidents play a significant role in deciding who is in line for the presidency.

Education

Educational level of trustees. Current community college trustees are well-educated individuals, with over 85 percent having earned the bachelor's degree or higher. Slightly more than one-half of the trustees have earned a graduate degree.

Educational level of presidents. As one would expect, presidents are well educated. Over 88 percent of the presidents have attained the doctorate, with almost an equal percentage possessing either the Ed.D. (45.1 percent) or the Ph.D. (43.4 percent). Another 2.5 percent hold professional degrees in fields such as law and medicine. The percentage of presidents whose highest educational level is the master's degree is 8.6 percent, a percentage that has declined from almost 12 percent in 1991 (Vaughan, Mellander, and Blois, 1994).

Observations and questions. Trustees and presidents are well-educated individuals. Indeed, it would seem that they must be well educated if they are to meet the expectations and needs of a society that is increasingly becoming more complex and more demanding. The educational level of trustees has implications in a number of areas. For example, there is much literature available today on the role of the president and trustee. As suggested later in this volume, the literature on the presidency (and trusteeship) provides one source of continuity from the past to the present. Certainly trustees are quite capable of reading, understanding, and applying what they read.

In the 1995 trustee survey, nearly 93 percent of the trustees responded that they receive most of their information from the president and his or her staff. What responsibility do presidents have to make sure that trustees are exposed to any number of approaches to governing and leading the community college? A common theme throughout this volume is that trustee development should be a priority for both president and trustees. What does the educational level of trustees say about the professional development of trustees? Surely most trustees, regardless of educational level, can understand the need for a formal orientation program for new trustees. Yet many boards do not have such programs.

Chapters Three and Six in this volume emphasize that trustees are lifelong learners. Do presidents approach them as such? Certainly, most of the time. But do professional development programs encompass complex theories and concepts commensurate with the educational level and adult status of trustees? Every president and every governing board should know the educational levels of the trustees and use that knowledge to advantage for both board and college.

Political Party

Trustees' political party preferences. Over 85 percent of the current trustees claim affiliation with one of the nation's two major political parties. Forty-three percent state that they are Republicans, 42 percent Democrats. Another 14 percent claim that they are independents. Regardless of party affiliation, 52 percent of the trustees say they are moderates, 35 percent state that they are conservatives, and 12 percent are liberals.

Presidents' political party preferences. Almost 73 percent of the presidents claim affiliation with the nation's two major political parties, with 47 percent stating that they are Democrats and almost 26 percent listing their political choice as Republican. Almost 27 percent of the presidents identify themselves as independents, almost double the percentage of trustees to list themselves as such. Regardless of party affiliation, 67 percent of the presidents claim to be moderates and 18 percent state that they are conservatives, while 15 percent claim to be liberals.

Observations and questions. The most important observation regarding governing boards is that the political makeup of community college governing boards puts to rest, at least partially, one of higher education's most revered and enduring myths: that the governing boards of institutions of higher education are dominated by aging white Republicans. Aging—somewhat; white—yes; Republicans—no.

Whereas more presidents are Democrats than Republicans, questions regarding the political party affiliation of presidents and trustees lie much deeper than "Which party?" and "How many?". Significant questions involve the relationship between their party affiliation and their decision making. Are local- or state-appointed trustees bound to serve the interests of the authorities who appointed them? Although elected trustees tend to run on a nonpartisan ticket, are their campaigns supported by their political party? Do elected trustees "owe" their political party something for its support? The relationship between politics and community college governance is very complex, and these questions only expose the tip of the iceberg. We believe, however, that education should be nonpartisan and that the decisions made by presidents and governing boards should be based upon the best interests of the students, the community, and the institution, not the best interests of political parties.

Community College Attendance and Teaching

Trustees and community college attendance and teaching. A number of trustees not only serve on their institutions' governing boards but also have attended and taught at a community college. Fifty-one percent of the trustees have attended a community college at some point in their lives. Approximately 4 percent of the trustees have taught full-time, and 18 percent part-time, at a community college.

Presidents and community college attendance and teaching. Over 36 percent of the current presidents attended a community college. A large percentage of presidents have also taught at a community college. Approximately 82 percent of the presidents have taught full-time (43 percent), part-time (39 percent), or both (2 percent) at a community college.

Observations and questions. Several contributors to this volume suggest that trustees and presidents should work as a team, sharing a common vision and goal. If affiliation with an institution strengthens one's support, commitment, understanding, and emotional attachment to a common philosophy and goals, then community colleges appear to be in good shape, for many trustees and presidents have deep ties to the community college. Trustees, especially, are often grateful for the opportunities the community college has given them to further their education, and therefore they want to give something back to the community through their service on the community college's governing board. Presidents often fulfill part of their professional role through teaching at the community college, thus getting the opportunity to gain a better understanding of the community college's commitment to teaching. Both trustees and presidents would seem to have ties that bind them to the community college, both philosophically and practically.

Stress

Trustees and stress. Slightly over 4 percent of the trustees rate serving on a community college's governing board as very stressful. Almost 38 percent view the service as moderately stressful, and the remaining 58 percent see service on the board as not stressful.

Presidents and stress. Slightly over 52 percent of the presidents view the presidency as a high-stress position. Over 46 percent say the position is moderately stressful, while 1.5 percent consider the presidency as a low-stress position. The 1991 survey of presidents reported that 53 percent of the presidents viewed the position as a high-stress position and 44 percent felt that the stress level was moderate. Three percent reported in 1991 that the stress level was low (Vaughan, Mellander, and Blois, 1994).

Observations and questions. Regardless of size, location, and governance structure, the community college is a complex organization. Individuals who lead complex organizations are subject to stress. It is little wonder, with the complexities facing the community college today, that over one half of the presidents view the presidency as a high-stress position. Even though trustees see their position as much less stressful than that of the presidency, trustees should nevertheless be sensitive to potential causes of stress, both for themselves and for presidents.

In Chapter Six, one trustee writes that the single most salient characteristic of community college boards in the last two decades has been change. What is the effect on presidents when boards change? Is it true, as noted later in this volume, that change is not accepted willingly by either boards or presidents? If so, how does one handle change? One thing that is almost sure to raise the stress level of most presidents is a "split board." Similarly, a crisis on campus tends to send the stress level upward for both trustees and presidents.

Almost every community college has a crisis lurking in its future. As the authors of Chapters Seven and Eight in this volume suggest, crises come in many forms. If boards and presidents handle a crisis poorly, one can expect the stress level of both trustees and presidents to rise rapidly, even to the point of hampering the functioning of the college. Can a college develop a plan for handling a crisis so as to prevent much future stress?

Certainly one way of decreasing stress for presidents and trustees is to build a foundation of trust between the board and the president. Does working together to create a shared vision for the college enhance the trust between presidents and trustees, thereby decreasing stress? If selecting a president is the most important single function of the governing board, the second most important role may well be seeing that the president functions in an environment that is physically, emotionally, and mentally healthy. Such an environment would keep stress within reasonable boundaries, assuring that neither trustees nor presidents become paralyzed by too much stress.

Conclusion

The descriptive data provided in this chapter offer selected characteristics of community college trustees and presidents as a means of gaining insight into how they may best work together. By evaluating the pertinence of the data to a given institution, and by asking questions raised by the data, trustees and presidents may be able to understand their roles more thoroughly and arrive at better-informed joint decisions. This initial overview sets the scene for subsequent chapters in this volume, in the context of specific college settings, to explore the deeper meaning of many of the questions raised by the data.

References

Houle, C. O. *Governing Boards: Their Nature and Nurture.* San Francisco: Jossey-Bass, 1989.

Nason, J. W. *The Nature of Trusteeship: The Role and Responsibilities of College and University Boards.* Washington, D.C.: Association of Governing Boards of Universities and Colleges, 1982.

Vaughan, G. B., Mellander, G. A., and Blois, B. *The Community College Presidency: Current Status and Future Outlook.* Washington, D.C.: American Association of Community Colleges, 1994.

Whitmore, L. A. "Results of a National Survey of Local Community College Trustees: Trustee Characteristics." *Trustee Quarterly,* Fall 1987, 14–23.

GEORGE B. VAUGHAN *is a professor of higher education at North Carolina State University in Raleigh. Prior to becoming a professor, he served as a community college president for seventeen years.*

IRIS M. WEISMAN *is a research and teaching associate with ACCLAIM at North Carolina State University in Raleigh and the former director of curriculum services for Pima Community College in Tucson.*

Collectively, America's community college presidents have done a remarkable job in serving vital community needs even as they have found it increasingly difficult to secure the necessary resources to accomplish the task. More than any others, three qualities deserve consideration as prerequisites to a successful community college presidency: personal adaptability, role flexibility, and sound judgment.

The Community College Presidency: Qualities for Success

David R. Pierce, Robert P. Pedersen

Ours is an era of great social change and personal uncertainty about what the future holds. The community college is not exempt from that change and uncertainty; in fact, it has helped transform the college presidency into a calling of high expectations, broad responsibility, and limitless challenges. As community colleges continue to grow larger and their functions increase in number and diversity, society turns more and more often to the community college for solutions to problems. Expectations for community college presidents have grown more complex, demanding, and even contradictory. Aptly described by a scholar and former community college president as "leaders on the edge" (Vaughan, 1989, p. 3), community college presidents are increasingly called upon by constituents to find solutions to unprecedented social problems, often through the application of untested strategies—and to do so with limited resources. As one rural community college president has observed, presidents are expected to make a dollar's worth of difference with a dime's worth of resources.

Yet the challenges facing today's community college president are not limited to the perennial problem of inadequate resources. Few other roles in American society make comparable day-to-day demands on an individual. A community college president is not simply a problem-solver. The president is also expected to meet a governing board's need for impartial and expert counsel; inspire faculty and staff in matters pertaining to curriculum and instruction; serve as a model of ethical behavior; and provide, as conditions warrant, vision for the entire community.

Some might look at the circumstances of community college presidents and focus on how remarkably few resources and tools they possess to satisfy expectations. Yet while it is true that most community college presidents do not have those advantages of office enjoyed by many university presidents—a large foundation to ensure financial flexibility, a small army of support staff to respond to any unexpected crisis, faculty tenure, and the "mystique" of prestige (Vaughan, 1989, p. 35) inherited from earlier centuries—it is no less true that community college presidents have accomplished, and continue to accomplish, tremendous good in response to growing societal needs and expectations.

The positive effects of presidential leadership are evident at virtually every turn, in communities of every size, location, and circumstance, although awareness of these accomplishments rarely spreads beyond community borders. Presidents have shown exceptional leadership in preserving student access to proximate, affordable, and comprehensive programs at a time when states seem more than willing to shift the financial burden of education onto students through wholesale tuition and fee increases. Through a variety of strategies, presidents have proven particularly effective in restraining tuition growth at community colleges. Even as tuition at many elite colleges and fees at state universities rise sharply, the average community college tuition remains less than $1,500 (Riche, 1996).

The State of the Literature

As one would expect, with the expanded importance of the presidential role has come increased interest by scholars in the characteristics and qualities of community college presidents. Between 1989 and 1995 alone, more than 150 books, monographs, articles, and reports were written about the community college presidency. A wide variety of specific topics were considered, ranging from the unique challenges faced by the presidents of small, rural community colleges (Reichard, 1995) to a presidential perspective on strategic marketing (Pappas and Shaink, 1994). The attributes, demographics, behaviors, ideals, and values of presidents are now a staple concern of graduate students, aspiring administrators, university professors, and even presidents themselves.

The value of this literature to community colleges and their effective management is substantial. If nothing else, these works represent a tremendous resource for sitting presidents, providing them with the tools with which they can perform at ever higher levels of competence. But beyond its immediate value, this literature better equips our graduate schools and other leadership development programs to pass on the vision, ideals, knowledge, and skills of today's community college leaders to their successors. In an era of continuous change, this literature offers one of the few sources of continuity for the community college presidents of tomorrow, giving them invaluable insights into the needs of communities and proven strategies for addressing those needs.

The Literature and Its Limitations: Overlooking Essential Presidential Qualities

Beyond its fairly steady growth, a review of the presidential literature reveals at least one important area of concern. As a body, this literature has become steadily narrower in its focus, with individual works focusing on specific skills or detailed methodologies for the management of change, just as it has shown a tendency to adopt the language of industrial management. In themselves, these trends are not a concern, for they do not necessarily detract from the overall value or relevance of this literature, except that they pose the very real danger that future community college presidents may not be introduced in any systematic fashion to the most basic, but not necessarily obvious, qualities upon which all effective presidencies will be based in the next century.

More than any others, three qualities deserve our consideration as prerequisites to a successful community college presidency. The first is *personal adaptability:* the ability of a community college president to move comfortably among the various constituencies and stakeholders with whom he or she must work in identifying and addressing community needs. The second is *role flexibility:* the ability to mediate among constituencies and stakeholders, finding those points of consensus that form the basis of interagency partnerships and similar forms of collaboration. It is through the exercise of role flexibility that a community college president can leverage limited institutional resources in collaboration with other community organizations, enhancing a community's overall effectiveness in solving its problems. The third and most important quality, *sound judgment,* is also the most personal and most difficult to acquire. Sound judgment is a president's ability to listen to a wide range of interests (which are frequently in conflict), weigh a college's options in responding to these interests, consider any resulting strategy both in terms of its resource impact and its ethical implications in light of the college's stated mission, and then act based on this assessment.

Adaptability

Community college presidents have set a standard for personal adaptability in responding to recent and rapid changes in the objective conditions of most community colleges. Evidence of this adaptability can be found in the response of community college presidents to changing student demographics. The establishment of such specialized services as day care centers, citizenship programs, small-business centers, and large developmental studies programs were all prompted by the needs of previously unserved students. Whereas the resources to sustain these programs and services have come from a variety of sources, the common thread that has given focus and direction to these progressive initiatives has been strong and consistent presidential leadership. The creation of these programs reflected the commitment by community college presidents to work with an array of constituencies that higher education had chosen to ignore for too long—from the physically challenged or dislocated worker to the displaced homemaker or recent immigrant. This commitment has institutionalized these initiatives, bringing them in from the margin of institutional life, to ensure continued access for those students most in need of the community college and its services.

Cohen and Brawer have recently pointed out the risk that a community college can run when it broadens the range of constituencies served. The enrollment of developmental students, to cite one example, has been seen by some as posing a danger to the integrity of a community college's academic curriculum (Cohen and Brawer, 1996). For one scholar, at least, this danger is so grave that he would have community colleges abandon developmental programs altogether and seek greater prestige and public acceptance through a more narrowly defined and academic curriculum (Dougherty, 1994). But community college presidents have, by their actions, rejected any call to abandon developmental education. Presidents continue to adapt community college programs and services in response to the objective conditions of their students and communities, setting aside narrow, self-interested concerns with institutional prestige and placing top priority on the larger public good.

Evidence of the personal adaptability of community college presidents can also be found in their advocacy of more participatory and team-based campus governance, a position that may appear to be in direct opposition to their own self-interest (Lorenzo and LeCroy, 1994; Spanbauer, 1996). Both individually and through such associations as the Presidents Academy of the American Association of Community Colleges, presidents have demonstrated an openness to governing models that value diversity and consensus and recognize that "in a complex work setting group effort improves efficiency and effectiveness" (Howdyshell, 1995, p. 61). Community college presidents have embraced the need to redefine their roles in keeping with the spirit of a more egalitarian age.

Role Flexibility

According to one community college president (Myran, 1995), the dynamic nature of our times demands that the successful community college president be flexible. Whereas in the not-too-distant past a community college could function to some extent independently, it is increasingly the rule that community colleges can continue to provide comparable services only through collaboration with other agencies, organizations, and businesses. Models to guide community colleges through the challenges of collaboration building are becoming a regular feature of the community literature.

Although not always solely responsible for nurturing broad-based collaborations within their communities, community college presidents are likely to continue to bear principal responsibility for this role. In an era of scarce resources, and until a history of trust develops among community agencies and other service providers, presidents should expect to play a leading role in nurturing these new relationships from conception to full implementation.

Sound Judgment

The third of the essential attributes of a successful president is judgment. More so than with adaptability and flexibility, judgment is both a skill and a gift. At a minimum, judgment requires that an individual possess both the skill to listen to a wide range of often discordant opinions and the gift to cull from diverse voices points of agreement and the basis for common action. Ideally presidents have ready access to information, the resources needed to carry out any decision, and the autonomy to make their decisions free of external pressure. But as an experienced president recognizes, the exercise of judgment in the real world of the modern community college must be made with incomplete information, without adequate resources, and often in a climate of conflict. Presidents are required to make hard choices among a range of equally attractive options, leading to tension in the life of a college and its community.

Contributing to this tension is a persistent misconception about the freedom of presidents to exercise their professional judgment. No president is free to act independently of external authority and its constraints and expectations. Formally, community college presidents are employees of their governing boards, and their capacity to act is defined by these boards through policy. Because of the substantial variation in the governing structures of community colleges across the nation, it is difficult to generalize about the relative latitude of community college presidents to exercise professional judgment. But in all cases, there are limits, and the failure of campus constituencies and even community stakeholders to acknowledge these limits can be an unfortunate source of tension.

There is another, if somewhat less obvious, tension that follows directly from the exercise of presidential judgment: the tension between a president's personal system of ethics and values and the demands of the presidency. Ethical dilemmas, as one president observed, are invariably part of institutional life, especially for a college president (Hankin, 1992). Ideally, there would be no conflict between the personal values of presidents and the expectations of their governing boards or major campus constituencies; however, such conflicts grow increasingly difficult to avoid as organizations gain complexity and the interests of external constituencies become increasingly important. By accepting that such conflicts may occur and making positive resolution of such conflicts an integral part of the institutional culture, boards can minimize this continuing source of tension in the work of presidents and remove a major obstacle to organizational change.

The Emerging Challenges

As we have argued, the challenges that community college presidents face are many, and the answers are neither obvious nor simple. To a great degree, these challenges derive from fundamental changes in the structure of American society, as it transitions from an industrial to an information-based economy. As one source of leadership notes, "The challenges confronting American society, now more than ever, must be met by exceptional leaders who can deal with change and revitalize the institutions of America" (Roueche, Baker, and Rose, 1989, p. 5).

From a national perspective, three challenges stand out as having the greatest likelihood of significantly impacting the work of community college presidents and their institutions.

Technology. The first of these challenges is found in the incredible (and seemingly unending) revolution in technology. Much has been written extolling the virtues of this revolution: the opportunity it provides the "place-bound" to connect with the larger society, more efficient commerce, and greatly enhanced access to careers through America's Job Bank (Johnson and Lobello, 1996). Widespread availability of coursework via the Internet is likely the next step in this evolution.

But presidents have a special responsibility to recognize that this is not an evolution without cost. Not all community colleges have the resources needed to make the fullest use of the Internet and other technologies, much less introduce wideband interactive videoconferencing. Additionally, in an era of finite funding, money that flows into technology may come at the expense of the traditional classroom, creating a potential body of opposition to any technological innovations among those faculty and staff who do not see their interests served by such expenditures. And finally, the technological revolution has the potential to undermine further that sense of shared experience integral to community life and the very ability of community colleges to identify and address critical community needs.

Competing Demands. The second challenge facing community college presidents is found in demographic trends that suggest the potential for conflict among several of the community college's core values. At some point, it seems likely that the community college's fundamental commitment to access may find itself at odds with its equally powerful and valid commitment to quality and accountability. A community college can extend its resources only so far; its capacity is finite. How community colleges weigh and balance these values makes unprecedented demands on the thoughtful, deliberative judgment of community college presidents. As colleges strengthen the standards that form the very foundation of an education's enduring value, presidents are called upon to find ways to avoid limiting access and opportunity while also providing the advanced education that is essential to success in the competitive workplace.

Changing Concept of Community. The third challenge facing community college presidents is to bring greater understanding to what it means to be the leader of a community-based institution. In an earlier time, what this concept meant was easily understood; communities were seen as discrete locations, encompassing a definite geographic area. In a global world economy, linked by the Internet, the connection between community and location could be severed. This is not a challenge with an immediately apparent solution;

much depends on the future direction of telecommunication developments. But neither should community college presidents presume that traditional notions of community, with their heavy emphasis on location, will survive into the next century. If for no other reason than the desire of state legislatures to reduce the cost of higher education through consolidation and technological substitution for traditional instruction, community college presidents should anticipate new concepts of community.

Conclusion

Collectively, America's community college presidents have done a remarkable job in serving vital community needs even as they have found it increasingly difficult to secure the necessary resources to accomplish the task. To a large degree, their success can be attributed to their personal adaptability, their role flexibility, and their sound judgment when faced with difficult choices and unexpected challenges. There is no reason to expect any fundamental improvement in the dilemmas faced by these men and women, but we should also have every confidence that community college presidents can, as they have in the past, meet the challenges that confront their colleges and their communities.

References

Cohen, A., and Brawer, F. *The American Community College*. (3rd ed.) San Francisco: Jossey-Bass, 1996.

Dougherty, K. *The Contradictory College*. Albany: State University of New York Press, 1994.

Hankin, J. "Academic Scruples: Faculty and Personnel Issues." In G. Vaughan and Associates (eds.), *Dilemmas of Leadership: Decision Making and Ethics in the Community College*. San Francisco: Jossey-Bass, 1992.

Howdyshell, L. "Team Building Leadership." In G. Myran, T. Zeiss, and L. Howdyshell (eds.), *Community College Leadership in the New Century*. Washington, D.C.: American Association of Community Colleges, 1995.

Johnson, L., and Lobello, S. (eds.). *The 21st Century Community College: Technology and the New Learning Paradigm*. White Plains, N.Y.: IBM, 1996.

Lorenzo, A., and LeCroy, N. *A Framework for Fundamental Change in the Community College: Creating a Culture of Responsiveness*. Warren, Mich.: Macomb Press, 1994.

Myran, G. "Leadership Pathways to the New Century." In G. Myran, T. Zeiss, and L. Howdyshell (eds.), *Community College Leadership in the New Century*. Washington, D.C.: American Association of Community Colleges, 1995.

Pappas, R., and Shaink, M. "Strategic Marketing: The President's Perspective." *Community College Journal*, 1994, *64* (6), 29–34.

Reichard, D. "The Small Rural Community College." *1994 and Beyond: One President's View*. New Directions for Community Colleges, no. 23. San Francisco: Jossey-Bass, 1995.

Riche, J. (ed.). *The 1996–97 AACC Annual*. Washington, D.C.: American Association of Community Colleges, 1996.

Roueche, J., Baker, G., and Rose, A. *Shared Vision: Transformational Leadership in American Community Colleges*. Washington, D.C.: American Association of Community Colleges, 1989.

Spanbauer, S. *Reengineering Education with Quality*. Indianapolis: USA Research Institute, 1996.

Vaughan, G. B. *Leadership in Transition: The Community College Presidency*. New York: American Council on Education; Macmillan, 1989.

DAVID R. PIERCE is the president of the American Association of Community Colleges.

ROBERT P. PEDERSEN lives in Maryland.

Whether they are appointed or elected, trustees require special skills and a clear understanding of the board's unique responsibilities. Trustees also need reliable resources as they grow in their role. What is the current status of trustee education programs? How can board members be encouraged to study trusteeship? What should a trustee education program cover, and how should it be delivered?

Orientation and Professional Development of Trustees

Gary Davis

As teaching institutions, community colleges set rigorous standards for the preparation of students and faculty alike. Ironically, however, recent research by Vaughan and Weisman (1995) reveals that only 14 percent of boards require new trustees to participate in a structured orientation to the board. For 70 percent of the boards, new trustee orientation is voluntary, and 16 percent of the boards do not provide new trustees with formal orientation. Where a formal orientation is provided, the college president and staff provide the orientation 86 percent of the time. Board chairs conduct 47 percent of the orientations. Outside experts or others conduct the orientation for 36 percent of the boards. (The percentages add up to more than 100 percent because sometimes orientation leadership is shared.)

Continuing professional development by board members is less universal. In the Vaughan and Weisman (1995) study, 60 percent of chairs said that their trustees regularly study local issues as part of a program for board development. Forty-three percent said their boards engage locally in the study of state issues, and 14 percent of chairs reported that their boards participate in regular discussions of national issues related to community college performance. Nearly one of every four colleges does not provide any local professional development programs for trustees.

When boards engage in local professional development, topics range from board-president relations to public relations for trustees. According to Vaughan and Weisman (1995), the most common topic for discussion is budget and financial management of the college. The next most discussed subjects are trustee roles and responsibilities and board-president relations, two closely related topics. Most orientations touch on goal setting (69 percent) and policy development (70 percent), although the study does not reveal whether the new trustee is taught to formulate goals and policies or only to respond to proposals from the president and staff. The latter is likely because, according to the study, curriculum and academic issues are addressed in about one-half the orientations, and about one-half deal with the college mission or strategic planning. It is difficult to see how a board could formulate a program of goal setting or direct the mission of the college unless it first understood the nature of the student body and the issues inherent in deciding a college's mission and strategy. How many boards *regularly address* questions of accountability such as those framed by Carver (1994): Whom are we serving? What good are we doing? What should such service cost?

On the other hand, some of Vaughan and Weisman's findings (1995) are encouraging. The ethics of trusteeship and college faculty relations are covered in 62 percent of new college trustee orientation sessions. Less frequently discussed topics include college history and enabling legislation, college personnel issues, characteristics of community college students, physical plant and facilities, fundraising strategies for trustees, government relations, organizational design, and public relations for trustees.

Moving beyond the local scene, the Texas Association of Community Colleges (1996) recently surveyed state community college associations to determine what trustee development and education programs they offer. Responses varied widely. When associations provide trustee training, they usually address questions related to board policy making, the responsibilities and role of the trustee, college mission, state laws and regulations, current issues and trends, and the budget. Some states provide no trustee development programming, relying instead on local college efforts and the offerings of the Association of Community College Trustees (ACCT), the American Association of Community Colleges (AACC), the Association of Governing Boards of Universities and Colleges (AGB), and other national groups.

Motivating Boards to Pursue Trustee Development

Board development happens when trustees are motivated to pursue it. By the same token, when disincentives abound, trustee development rarely occurs. What incentives work? Encouragement by the trustee's patrons helps. Trustees join boards in one of three ways: some are appointed by their state's governor, some by local officials, and still others are elected. No matter how they are chosen, most trustees feel a real sense of loyalty to those who have given them the opportunity to serve. Whether trustees enthusiastically embrace opportunities for trustee orientation and development depends, in part, on what their patrons expect of them. If those who played a significant role in the selection of the trustee signal an interest in the new board member's growth and development, the trustee is inclined to participate in professional development activities. If the voters or appointing officials do not seem to be interested in the new trustee's professional development, the development may not take place.

In states where trustees are appointed, those who are responsible for making the appointments can contribute to the board's development by making clear to each appointee that much is expected of each trustee. When the governor's office, the board of education, or the county commission asks the new trustee to commit to a program of trustee education, the new board member is likely to comply.

The views of the news media can also influence trustee attitudes toward their own professional development. Because political considerations often affect the appointment of trustees, reporters and editors usually take an interest in both trustee selection and board behavior. Editors can be asked to show support for the efforts of trustees who work to improve their performance. The media can also be asked to recognize the many hours that conscientious trustees sacrifice in order to discharge their public trust.

Perhaps the strongest incentive for trustee development is the trustee's own self-concept. When trustees see themselves as leaders of a learning organization, they tend to believe that the college and the community need a clear signal from the board that *everyone's* professional development is important. As lifelong learners, board members can be role models and establish professional development expectations in others. Often the new trustee has already discovered the advantages of continuing education either at work or by serving on another board. By reflecting on their experiences in successful organizations, trustees can recall the exhilaration that comes from being part of a well-trained, winning team. Organizations excel only when their members are well trained and when roles and responsibilities are clearly understood.

College presidents can also encourage trustee orientation and development. Presidents often meet with new trustees at the time of appointment. Although the president's first meeting with the trustee is often devoted to the task of establishing a strong social relationship, the president can use the occasion to praise board development activities and to encourage board members to get involved in state and national trustee associations. In general, trustees have a high degree of respect for college presidents. If thorough and effective trustee orientation is a high priority for the college president, chances are that it is a high priority for the trustee as well.

When new trustees are elected or appointed, the president and board chair cannot afford to wait for the new trustee to ask for an orientation. It must be offered—and even required. When the trustee is slow in accepting the offer, the president and board chair must continue to point out the advantages of an orientation. Although the best orientations begin before the new trustee has attended her or his first board meeting, a delayed orientation is better than none at all. Even if it is put off for several weeks or several months, an orientation and introduction to key areas of knowledge for trustees can be an invaluable tool for a relatively new board member.

Boards themselves can strongly encourage orientation and development of trustees. The board of Iowa Western Community College, for example, has adopted a formal policy requiring orientation and "conferences concerning procedure" (Iowa Western Community College, 1994). Some other boards have adopted policies that clearly state the board's expectation that each of its members pursue some program of trustee development.

Ultimately, boards themselves are responsible for trustee development. Although presidents can encourage trustee development, the natural tension between board and president may require that someone other than the president take the lead. The "someone," of course, is the board itself. Along with the president, the board chair can use the office to encourage new trustees to take advantage of orientation and development opportunities. Yet the responsibility for board development does not fall only on the president and the chair. Because their development serves to improve the whole board, all trustees bear the responsibility for seeing that they continue to grow in their roles.

The Importance of Effective Presentation

Because each board is unique, one trustee development program cannot fit all boards. Those designing professional development programs for trustees would also profit by considering the *particular circumstances of the college and the new board member.* Does the college, for example, have a tradition of providing and encouraging educational activities for its trustees? If so, the program can take advantage of this tradition by sharing it with the new trustee. If not, some explanation of the program's importance is required. If the college has a strong department of continuing education or contract training, trustees can be informed of the organizational advantages of training for everyone in the organization.

Is the college located close to other colleges that also encourage board development opportunities? If so, colleges can economize by sharing resources and curriculum. Can some of the training be outsourced to state or national trustee associations? Are a number of the trustees relatively new in their roles? If so, they could be taught as a group. Although trustees do not have to be friends in order to work together effectively, board deliberations improve when trustees understand something about each other's experiences and personality traits. In particular, board productivity increases when trustees understand that each member has his or her own style of behavior. Boards can profit from a retreat in which each trustee discovers his or her own personality type and the strengths and weaknesses that attach to each type. For example, effective boards value intuitive thinking as well as analysis that is based strictly on hard evidence. Similarly, both the deliberate and the eager trustee have a role to play on a well-balanced board. Once trustees develop an appreciation of several styles of behavior, their understanding of their board colleagues often increases and board relations improve.

If the board lacks experienced members, a trustee development program can be designed to enhance leadership and expose all trustees to vital chapters in the college's recent history. If the board is already dominated by very experienced trustees, attention can be paid to their needs and the challenges that new trustees face as they attempt to break into a well-established lineup. Is the college in dire financial straits? If so, the educational program for trustees should be developed with great concern for its costs. If, on the other hand, the college enjoys good funding, special opportunities for board development can be considered. Is the college heavily dependent on state funding? If so, the trustee development program can be tailored to prepare trustees for the task of increasing the state's level of support. If the college is primarily funded from local sources, training can focus on the task of serving local constituencies, thereby strengthening the college's financial base.

Trustee development should also reflect individual characteristics of each board member. What is the trustee's self-concept? Is she or he self-directed or directed by external forces? If the latter, how can those forces be used to encourage training? If the trustee responds primarily to external forces, the persons responsible for the appointment should receive briefings on the objectives of trustee training and the new trustee's progress. If board members are elected, press releases can inform the public of the board member's achievements and increase the likelihood that the trustee takes advantage of future training opportunities.

How well do trustees understand the jargon of education and finance? A good glossary of terms is always appreciated, for it helps the trustee avoid asking a question that reveals ignorance. Those who design the trustees' curriculum should continuously monitor the background of new trustees so that the training fits their educational background and life experiences.

How important are spouse and family to the trustee's decision about participating in trustee education? If the answer is "very important," some family activities should be planned in conjunction with trustee training sessions. What are the ethnic and ethical sensitivities of the new trustees? Sometimes board members test trustee development programs for sensitivity to their values and heritage. The more that professional development program designers and trainers know about what is important to trustees, the more effective the training is.

How much time do trustees have for their development? Many trustees are very busy people. Would they prefer "drive-in" seminars that can be attended in a single day without spending a night away from home? Would delivery of instruction over the Internet or by fax be convenient and effective? Or do the trustees want an opportunity to invest more time with trustees from other colleges facing similar problems? Every board is different; the wise president and board chair monitors the trustees for current answers. How politically experienced are the new trustees? Some trustees come straight from the world of politics while others have no working knowledge of how laws are made. If trustees are to be effective advocates for their colleges, their political skills must be sharpened and then synchronized.

How has the new trustee been trained to think? Trustees' past training and experience sometimes lure them into viewing college issues with a single focus. For example, attorneys who join the board may see the college only in light of the law, when in fact financial, ethical, and educational issues should also be raised. Teachers who join boards are often tempted to see every issue only in terms of its educational ramifications, even though boards must also attend to the requirements of finance and the law. Good trustee development encourages trustees to use a variety of lenses to view college issues. Board topics are seldom so simple that a single approach suffices.

A Model Trustee Education Curriculum

Whatever program of professional development is chosen, it should fit the use to which it is put by the trustee. In order to be good board members, what do trustees need to know? What skills do boards need in order to be successful guardians of the institutions they govern?

Learning the Board's Culture. Like anyone in a new role, the new trustee has questions. Some of the questions are personal. The new board member is not likely to wonder aloud, "How do I fit into this group?" and "Do I have what it takes to be a good trustee?" Effective orientation reassures new trustees and helps them feel more comfortable with their new responsibilities and their new colleagues on the board. Because initial impressions endure, an early and effective orientation can build a strong foundation for future trustee interactions.

To begin, new trustees need to understand the style, habits, structure, and procedures of the board that they are about to join. Without an adequate orientation, new trustees can learn their board's style and habits only through painstaking, personal observation. Such study sometimes takes months or years, and during that time the new trustee is likely to be heard only occasionally during board meetings. New trustees want to know how the board is accustomed to operating. Do board members meet only when the board is in session, or do they also meet for study, or for social occasions? What are the habits of the board? Which trustee is used to doing which job? Is trustee development shared by all, or is it the private domain of one or two board members? How much time and money is the board comfortable in spending on its own activities? What should a board member do if he or she must miss a meeting? What events at the college are trustees expected to attend? Should they let the president know if they plan to visit the campus? How should trustees react to complaints about the college?

As Anderson and LaVista (1994) have noted, these are questions that run through the minds of new trustees. But new board members usually are hesitant to verbalize such questions, which are seldom, if ever, found on the agenda of a formal board orientation session. By discussing the board's traditions and culture during a new trustee's orientation, the president and board chair can help the trustee understand and adapt to the board that she or he is joining.

The board's formal procedures should also be addressed. New board members should be given an opportunity to provide input on questions of when and how often the board meets. Sometimes the board's traditional schedule does not fit the professional or work schedule of the new trustees. New trustees should be told the procedures that board members must follow in order to place an issue on the board agenda. They also deserve to know who decides whether the board has committees and who serves on each committee. What are the policies of the board, and how can they be amended?

During the orientation of new members, the subject of closed sessions can also be discussed. The damage that comes from leaks can be squarely addressed, and examples of legal jeopardy arising from inappropriate discussion of closed discussions can be shared. New board members are more likely to respect the rules of closed sessions when they have personally discussed the damage that broken confidences can create. In other words, it is easier to keep confidences when one understands precisely why they are important.

In addition to a briefing on the board's own procedures (including closed-session procedures), the orientation should cover certain other important topics. In his study of private college boards, Chait (1993) found that colleges benefit from effective boards and that effective boards are populated by trustees with competencies in six key areas. A good professional development program, therefore, nurtures these traits in each trustee: (1) appreciation of the college's context or history and current setting, (2) curiosity and an appetite for trustee education, (3) familiarity with effective group process techniques, (4) inclination to engage in step-by-step, logical analysis, (5) interest in communicating with key college constituencies, and (6) appreciation of strategic planning. Each trait deserves some comment, since each contributes directly to the effectiveness of the board.

An Appreciation of the College's Context. When community colleges began nearly one hundred years ago, they were designed primarily to prepare students for the last two years of university work leading to a bachelor's degree. Experiential learning, distance learning, collaborative and cooperative learning, self-paced learning, and computer assisted learning were subjects yet to be discovered. Today several educational theories compete for the attention of community college faculty and staff. In order to understand issues that often divide people within the college, board members need to have some understanding of the current theories that undergird community college education.

Educational theories change over time. Lacking familiarity with the institution's recent history, new trustees often struggle to understand the college's current educational orientation. When someone joins a board, several projects are in motion; and when she or he leaves the board, the same is true. Most trustees do not enjoy the privilege of serving on the college's first board. Many issues have been faced, many commitments have been made, and many lessons have been learned before the new trustee attends the first meeting. To be effective in their roles, new trustees must learn something about the history of their board and the college it serves. Presidents can provide them with copies of minutes of the previous year's board meetings and summaries of the college's recent performance. A list of trends may also be important. For example, a 2 percent decline in enrollment may not be significant—unless it follows similar declines in each of the last ten years.

If the president has not provided copies of recent minutes or any historical data on the college, new trustees can ask about the history of the college and the board. If a history of the college has been produced, new trustees should receive it. Presidents and board chairs can often arrange social events to give new trustees the benefit of conversations with people who have observed the college's growth and development over many years. By interacting informally and frequently with experienced board members and other college representatives, new trustees learn the values, norms, and prevailing practices of the institution. Only then can they accept the college's traditions or begin to constructively challenge them.

In examining the college's recent history, board members should be alert to any failures by the college to respond to changes within the community. How is the community changing, and what problems and opportunities do those changes bring? How can the community college help solve the problems? How is the ethnic and social mix of the district changing? Often trustees see the district as it is or was, rather than as it may become. Boards need to learn to scan the environment to identify trends that point to the future. This is particularly important if the board fails to reflect new or emerging populations within the district. When board vacancies occur, should they be filled by people from underrepresented groups? Boards can use conversations with those seeking to become trustees to explain the college and to listen to new voices and new views. Is the board willing to hire a college president who differs from them in gender, race, place of origin, or age but who fits the district's population? Could such a president lead the college more effectively than someone whose social profile closely resembles that of the board?

An Appetite for Trustee Education. In order to be an inspiration to the learning organization that it governs, the board needs a plan for its own education. Chait (1993) found that ineffective boards generally refuse to learn and that they may reject assessments of their own performance. Good boards, on the other hand, seek to discover how well they are performing, and when improvement is needed they institute learning opportunities for their members. College presidents and senior board members can use a variety of methods to interest new trustees in their professional development. When senior board members and the president express clear and high expectations for the new trustee, the new board member's performance is enhanced.

Familiarity with Effective Group Process. Related closely to the board's understanding of its own educational needs is an appreciation of the key elements of effective group process. Good boards understand the need for efficient and effective discussion before reaching a decision. A working knowledge of parliamentary procedure and good personal relationships among trustees can create a climate for healthy discussion. Effective boards include members with a variety of styles. Some push rapidly toward decisions, for example, while others are more deliberate. A balance of styles contributes to a healthy group process and good decisions.

Of course, a variety of styles can occasionally create tension on the board. When differing approaches among the trustees clash, boards can benefit from ground rules for deliberation, like those suggested by (and paraphrased here from) the work of Schwarz (1994):

- Test assumptions and inferences.
- Share all relevant information.
- Focus on interests, not positions.
- Be specific and use examples.
- Agree on what important words mean.
- Explain the reasons behind one's statements, questions, and actions.
- When you must disagree with a member of the group, disagree openly.
- Make statements; then invite questions and comments.
- Jointly design ways to test disagreements and solutions.
- Be willing to tackle all timely and important issues.
- Keep the discussion focused.
- Do not take cheap shots or distract the group.
- Expect all members to participate in all phases of the process.
- Keep appropriate nongroup members informed of what they need to know.
- Make decisions by consensus, if possible.
- Conduct self-critiques.

Effective group discussion and decision making requires that all group members respect themselves and each other. Trustees who develop the skills involved with effective group process are more confident when voicing their own opinions and, at the same time, work to ensure that all voices on the board are heard.

Talent for Analytical Decision Making. Trustees must resist the temptation to rush into decisions without the benefit of thorough understanding and careful analysis of issues. The best boards use a variety of tested methods to identify and solve problems. New trustees should be encouraged during their orientation session to test their preconceptions against information that the college can provide. Sometimes a new trustee can alert the board to serious problems that it has overlooked. At other times, however, the trustee's notion that the college is failing in a given area may not stand up under careful scrutiny of the evidence. Although intuition sometimes plays a role in good board work, it can never be a substitute for good research and analysis.

Interest in Key College Constituencies. The board holds the college in trust for the community. In order to determine what the community expects of the college, trustees should find a way to tap the opinion of the true owners of the college. When community members seem unaware of the college and the work of the board, trustees should devise a method for increasing the visibility of both. For those who follow the trustees' work closely, the board should strive to communicate carefully its agenda and decisions. Without an intentional program of board public relations or communications, rumors reign and trustees lose control of the information flow. Every board should have a plan for communicating with the public. Discussions with key constituencies should not be left to chance or to the public-comment section of the board agenda. Rather, the board should plan several discussions each year with constituents and make an effort to inform the public regularly of key board decisions and developments.

College trustees need the help of the president and the college public relations officer in their effort to aid public understanding of the role and contributions of the board. New trustees should be cautioned not to speak independently; if they do, some members of the press and the community may misconstrue their comments as a statement of the board's position. In order to avoid such confusion, the board chair and the president are usually commissioned to speak for the board, and new trustees need to understand both the rule and the reasons behind it. If trustees do speak independently, they owe it to the board to emphasize that their comments are not to be taken as a reflection of the board's position. They should also emphasize that only the board has the legal power of governance and that individual trustees have no authority at all.

New trustees may show a tendency to follow the winds of community opinion, wherever they blow. In orientation of new trustees and during continuing professional development sessions, board members should challenge one another to lead in developing positive, constructive community opinion. As professional politicians have long realized, elected and appointed officials can participate in the shaping of public opinion. By sharing information and by leading discussions of vital issues, board members can show community members how to solve community problems.

Appreciation of Strategic Planning. Finally, the board should develop a taste for strategic thinking. By concentrating on long-range strategies, the board can plan for the future by taking advantage of the college's strengths and minimizing its weaknesses. When they are engaged in strategic decision making, trustees should take note of threats from the college's competitors and understand opportunities that new social conditions provide. The objective of strategic thinking is to provide the college with competitive advantages and to prevent problem areas from becoming threats to the institution's viability.

Board members must learn how to ask presidents for information that enables trustees to compare the college's performance with the performance of its peers in such key areas as drawing power; student and faculty diversity; program variety; instructional effectiveness; physical plant adequacy; tuition and fees; student support services; philanthropy; and obtaining local, state, and federal support. Tools to teach strategic planning skills to trustees are available. One of the best is the AGB's *Strategic Decision Making: Key Questions and Indicators for Trustees* (n.d.). Another is the AACC's *Community Colleges: Core Indicators of Effectiveness* (1994).

Although regular board meetings often involve discussion of urgent issues, more important and complex problems usually are not addressed at these sessions. Strategic thinking often emerges in board retreats, when the trustees have enough time to explore large and complex issues facing the college. During retreats, trustees and the president have sufficient time to review their past performance and plan changes that enable trustees to think strategically throughout the year.

Resources for Trustees

Trustees need a continuous flow of information about the colleges they govern. The college can provide a subscription to periodicals such as *Community College Times, Community College Week, The Chronicle of Higher Education, ACCT Quarterly,* and *Change.* Many sources are available via the Internet and through the college library. Some boards develop collections of books as well as other materials for trustees to borrow.

Conclusion

In business and in the public sector, boards increasingly must account for the value that they take from the organization. When a board returns more to a college than it takes, it can be classified as a good investment for the people of the district. Trustees want to provide a good return on time and money invested in their board. Only through a program of professional development can trustees assure their board's accountability. By mastering their role and responsibilities, board members can ensure that their colleges continue to be higher education's best avenue to the American dream.

References

American Association of Community Colleges. *Community Colleges: Core Indicators of Effectiveness.* Washington, D.C.: American Association of Community Colleges, 1994.

Anderson, R., and LaVista, D. J. "Survival Skills and the Trustee Orientation." *Trustee Quarterly,* Fall 1994, pp. 2–4.

Association of Governing Boards of Universities and Colleges. *Strategic Decision Making: Key Questions and Indicators for Trustees.* Washington, D.C.: Association of Governing Boards of Universities and Colleges, n.d.

Carver, J. *A New Vision of Board Leadership: Governing the Community College.* Washington, D.C.: Association of Community College Trustees, 1994.

Chait, R. P. *The Effective Board of Trustees.* Phoenix, Ariz.: Oryx Press, 1993.

Iowa Western Community College. *Board Policy 203.1.* Council Bluffs: Iowa Western Community College, December 19, 1994.

Schwarz, R. *The Skilled Facilitator.* San Francisco: Jossey-Bass, 1994.

Texas Association of Community Colleges. *Training Survey.* Unpublished. Austin: Texas Association of Community Colleges, 1996.

Vaughan, G. B., and Weisman, I. M. Community college trustee study (untitled). Unpublished raw data, 1995.

GARY DAVIS is the executive director of the Illinois Community College Trustees Association in Springfield.

Trust is the key to positive and productive board-president relations. Just as each community college is different, so is each president and trustee. Build on the foundation of respect and integrity, find the style that is the most successful for the individuals involved, and adapt.

Board-President Relations: A Foundation of Trust

Norm Nielsen, Wayne Newton

Community colleges face a mighty challenge: to develop the full potential of the country's greatest resource, its human resource. To do so, the board and president must work in harmony to develop a common vision that brings to reality the hopes and dreams of the American public.

Most community college trustees and presidents would agree that mutual trust is key to successful board-president relations, as well as to the success of the institution. Board members must trust the president to operate the college on a daily basis. On the other hand, the president must trust that the board has the integrity to guide the future of the college based on accurate information.

The question, then, is how to develop and maintain trust. A climate of trust requires many traditionally honored human characteristics: honesty, openness, integrity, and humility, to name a few. With those qualities as a foundation, quality leadership, team building, and planning and organization on behalf of both the board and the president enhance and maintain their relationship.

Leadership

Effective leaders help articulate common goals and focus efforts on a college's unique needs.

A Shared Vision and Mission: Building a Bridge. Sometimes trustees wonder why so much of their precious time is lost to tasks such as writing vision and mission statements. A board member once asked about such a task, "Why doesn't somebody write it so that we can all get back to work?" Many trustees come to realize, however, that when writing vision or mission statements, *more important than the results is the process itself*. As board members express themselves, defining concepts through words, they develop a precious sense of ownership. With a concisely worded mission statement, the growth of the college becomes a matter of turning the pages of a well-defined plan.

Through the process of developing a mission statement, a bridge is built between the president and the board, and between the board and the college's divergent constituencies. In any community, trustees come from many different backgrounds and experiences. Trustee diversity is a strength if the board is to understand the needs of its various audiences. Through the process of developing a mission statement, trustees and presidents address such thorny questions as, "How can an all-male board relate to women's groups and issues?" and "Can a board composed primarily of farmers connect in a significant way with hospitals, public agencies, and the business community?" It is essential that community college board members and presidents examine and understand who they represent. The best way for trustees to do this is by taking a hard look at themselves—who they are and who they are not—and then determining how to fill the inevitable voids that occur.

Whereas the board of trustees and the president have separate leadership roles at a community college—one in policy, the other in administration—they must share a vision for the college's role in the community and for its future. Establishing a shared vision begins at the point of presidential selection.

Selecting a President. Choosing a person who fits the leadership needs of the community college is one of the board's most important functions. The importance of this task merits involving college staff and perhaps professional consultants in establishing job qualifications and desirable characteristics.

A presidential vacancy should be looked at as an opportunity to rededicate the college to the community. The internal and external family should ask the question, "Where do we go from here?" The board should then proceed to find the person with the qualifications to advance the college in a way that reflects the interests of the community.

When a good match has been established among the board, president, and college, retention becomes an important issue. Certainly, a good working relationship and mutual, realistic expectations between the board and president contribute to developing and maintaining an ongoing, shared vision that favors presidential retention.

Expectations. Throughout the tenure of any president, but certainly at the start of presidential appointment, the board must communicate clearly the expectations that it holds for the president. Lack of clear transmission of expectations from the board to the new president can be disastrous. At one community college, the trustees decided that their institution needed a major overhaul and hired a president on that premise. The new president understood his mandate to "sweep with a new broom" and went swiftly to work. The sweeping changes reached the media in no time, and the community began to look at the college with renewed scrutiny. In this instance, the board chose to disavow responsibility for the decisions made by the new president; the result was a barrage of criticism of the president that weakened his ability to lead.

The lesson to be learned here is that beginning with the hiring of a new president, the board should deliver formal, written expectations. Ideally, these criteria should be presented annually with objective benchmarks for measurement. These expectations, intended to reflect the mission and future direction of the college, will prove invaluable for the presidential performance evaluations to follow.

Presidential Evaluations. The process of presidential evaluations varies from college to college, but in all cases the task should be performed by the board rather than the community or employees. Evaluations must be handled with sensitivity and performed in the best interest of the college. The results of the evaluation should motivate the president to focus on the tasks to be accomplished and to choose what is right for the institution, rather than what is easy or popular. Presidential evaluation should include a review of planning, budgeting and finance, facilities, curriculum, community needs, public relations, and personnel.

Open and honest input on presidential performance from each board member is essential. Trustees should therefore have a voice regarding the design of the process through which their input is shared. When legally permitted, an executive session of the board may be desirable to facilitate open discussion of presidential performance. Through another mechanism, individual board members submit written comments to the chair, who then compiles and summarizes them. Some additional guidelines for presidential evaluation follow:

Evaluation should enhance and strengthen presidential performance. Both praise and criticism should be used cautiously, allowing neither a disappointing situation nor an exemplary one to sway the entire process.

The basis for evaluation should be a shared vision between the president and the board as well as compliance with the job description.

The evaluation of the president reflects on the board. The trustees must share responsibility for the president's failures along with credit for the president's successes.

Evaluation should be in writing and conducted separately from contract renewal and salary adjustments.

Consistency is the key. When a number of people are performing a detailed evaluation, it has an inherent tendency to be subjective. A specific, thorough, and objective evaluation instrument with adequate room for discussion can minimize confusion.

The board should never ask the staff to evaluate the president, even if there appear to be problems. If the president would like to be reviewed by employees, their comments should not be shared with the board.

When the college is running smoothly, the president and the board may feel a formal evaluation is not necessary. Nothing could be further from the truth. Properly executed evaluations serve the needs of the college, president, and board and are essential to a positive relationship and mutual understanding.

Trustee Evaluation. Evaluation of trustees, either as a board or individually, promotes open communication and shared vision just as evaluation of a president does. The electorate or appointing official is, of course, the final evaluator of the performance of a trustee. Generally, however, this type of evaluation comes about only after a situation of some severity occurs. A February 1996 survey showed that only 14 percent of college presidents evaluate their board (League for Innovation in the Community College, 1996). This is an underutilized opportunity for relationship building and problem resolution.

Like presidents, good chairs are hard to find and should be retained whenever possible. Rotation of the board chair is an unnecessary disruption when board meetings are running smoothly and there is good rapport between the president, chair, board, and staff. However, if term limits are not in place and the chair is no longer performing well, trustees are often reluctant to take action. Therefore, an annual review mechanism must be in place. As with evaluations of the president, the review should not be foregone for any reason—even success.

Contract Negotiations. For a president, the employment contract can also be the basis for stability. Boards seeking to attract or retain peak performers should offer a multiple-year contract, if the law allows. Such a contract encourages innovation and risk taking, whereas a president on a one-year contract may be tempted to play it safe to ensure renewal. On the other hand, community college boards are becoming more vulnerable to large financial settlements if a president's multiyear contract is broken. For this reason, a contract severance agreement can provide the balance between board protection and presidential job security.

The board chair must provide leadership in offering a competitive and reasonable contract. A candidate for president often avoids the subject of salary and other benefits rather than risk media attention or the appearance of greed. Board chairs benefit from knowledge of what contract stipulations are found at comparable schools. State and national community college associations can be of assistance in this matter.

The sensitivity of contract discussions has led some presidents to seek representation by an attorney for the negotiation. The objectivity of this arrangement may minimize the potential for divisive disagreements; however, some boards may see the presence of an attorney as excessively formal. For this reason, such an arrangement should be mutually agreed upon.

Transition Plans. Even in the best of situations, change is inevitable. Retirement, relocation, or other factors affect the makeup of the board-and-president leadership team. According to one study, the average number of years that trustees have currently served is approximately eight and one-half. Slightly more than half (51 percent) of the trustees have served for six years or less, and slightly less than half (49 percent) have served from seven years to over thirty. Terms of appointments for most trustees range from three to six years in length, although most trustees can serve unlimited terms (Vaughan and Weisman, 1995).

By contrast, more than half (55 percent) of community college presidents have served in their present position for six years, approximately 25 percent for seven to ten years, and the final 25 percent for up to thirty-one years. Nearly 30 percent of all presidents have held a presidency at more than one institution (Vaughan and Weisman, 1996).

In 1988, it was found that 15–20 percent of all trustees were in the first year of their appointment to the board (American Association of Community Colleges, 1988). A review of the AACC membership directories from 1991 through 1995 reveals that, on average, approximately 10 percent of community college presidencies are filled each year (Vaughan, 1995). The data reveal that although some presidents and trustees enjoy long relationships with their institutions, there is a sizable amount of turnover among presidents and the trustees.

Whenever possible, departing presidents or board members should give or be given sufficient notice prior to exiting to allow the board time for planning for replacements. Although selection and orientation procedures are lengthy, costly, and involved, they are made easier with planning and are always worth the effort. Some governing boards have created written plans for leadership transition. This is particularly common in cases where the board is pleased with the status and direction of the institution. A transition plan should also include plans for orientation and education of new board members. Occasionally, recruitment of trustees—based on their interest, involvement, and commitment to the community and the college—is advisable. A transition plan assists the board in maintaining institutional stability, even during a time of change in board membership.

Team Building

Disparate individuals come together to work effectively as a team when they build on a foundation of mutual trust and respect.

Reaching Out. True teams operate on trust. They trust that each member is making a contribution and acting with integrity, in the best interest of the group and the cause. Each member of a team is responsible for maintaining and building the team spirit. On a community college board of trustees, team building is important at all times, and particularly when a new member joins the group. Reaching out to newcomers prevents alienation, or the formation of "new" and "old" factions. Social activities, retreats, conferences, and seminars allow time for informal conversation as well as more in-depth and confidential discussions about the college. Group dinners before or after board meetings provide an excellent opportunity for board members and selected administrators to get to know one another.

Levels of Involvement. A president and chair can build a team that allows each trustee to choose his or her level of involvement. The board chair sets the tone for meetings and can steer away from contentious discussions over administrative matters, while encouraging communication to understand critical issues, solve problems, and build support. The president, on the other hand, can ensure that all trustees are equally informed and should provide rec-ommendations based on detailed knowledge of college programs, budgets, and trends, as well as personal experience. Such recommendations should be reviewed based on their own merits, though, and not solely on what is pro-moted by the president.

Committees. Committee work offers several advantages to meetings of the full board. Board members may use their time more efficiently through committees, and they can avail themselves of individual expertise or interest. However, in some cases appointment of board committees can threaten team-building efforts. Formation of committees may require the chair to single out board members, and appointment to a committee may be perceived as an invi-tation to meddle in college affairs. It is tempting to use the talents and exper-tise of trustees. However, problems can ensue when the lawyer on the board becomes the college attorney, the banker chairs the finance committee, or a trustee from a minority group is expected to have all the answers regarding the college minority population.

Furthermore, combined committees of staff and trustees can be intimidat-ing for the staff and can leave trustees feeling uninformed. The board should rely on the staff and president for expertise and respond to their reports and recommendations while in full session. Similarly, a president should avoid con-tacting a single board member for opinions or involvement. In general, if a deci-sion merits board involvement, it merits the involvement of the entire board.

Task forces, a useful alternative to committees, are small groups that meet to accomplish a goal and disband when the task is completed. Task forces should deal only with such issues as policy review, board leadership, board vacancies, ethics statements, and social events. They should not be used for issues dealing with human relations, finance, or facilities management.

Teamwork. Every community college has its student success stories. Until trustees feel the heartbeat of the college—as expressed through the suc-cesses of the students—they will not fully appreciate the college's role in devel-oping human capital. Presenting trustees with examples of student successes develops a sense of appreciation for the mission that the college and the trustee must now share. Tell them about the mother of two who now supports herself as a legal assistant because of coursework at the college or the displaced worker who turned from meat-packer to truck driver. Other examples abound. Pres-idents who expose their trustees to a generous dose of the human growth that we have all witnessed on community college campuses very quickly turn crit-ics into advocates.

A sense of commitment and ownership from trustees contributes to team-work. Many factors contribute to commitment and ownership, among them knowledge of students and staff, the sharing of responsibility for failure and credit for successes, and longevity. Trustees who are alumni of the institution, or of any community college, often come with a sense of commitment. Famil-iarity with students and staff can be developed through presentations by departments on a rotating basis at each board meeting.

When serving as a welcoming committee for trustees, college leaders present the best evidence of trust between the president and his or her team. Board meetings should be held on campus, and trustees should be encouraged to arrive early, shop in the bookstore, eat in the cafeteria, or simply walk the grounds. Knowing the college and its students can be one of the greatest rewards of trusteeship. Campus newsletters, magazines, or articles about the college in the local newspaper should also be shared, as should minutes of advisory committee meetings. This information provides the trustee with an opportunity to see the college from an outsider's perspective.

Knowledge about the college mission and involvement of the trustees also contribute to the team spirit. Workshops, seminars, conferences, and state and national meetings, although an expense to the district, are educational and well worth the investment. These occasions also build the board member's pride in the institution, are an opportunity to visit with trustees from other colleges, and allow for some cheerleading—using the human-interest stories heard at board meetings. When possible, the president or a senior administrator should accompany the board to these events. Board members should also be involved in their community's clubs and service organizations as a way of staying informed and receiving feedback about the college.

Planning and Organization

Predictability invites trust. For a community college board, evidence of predictability can be found in trustee handbooks, a regular board agenda, an annual calendar of discussion items, timely board packets, scheduled retreats and conferences, and annual evaluation of president and trustees. An annual calendar should be based on required budgeting activities. This sample calendar is based on a fiscal year running from July 1 through June 30:

- Annual meeting and board nominations: July
- Election of trustees: September
- Organization of board: October
- Retreat and orientation of new trustees: November
- Review of mission: December through March
- Evaluation of president, board, and board chair: February
- Approval of budget: February through March
- Faculty contracts: April
- Review of presidential contract: May
- Review, revision, and updating of policy: Biannually or as needed
- Reports from departments, personnel items, and financials: All meetings

Retreats. Regular board retreats offer trustees, particularly new board members, an opportunity to get acquainted in a relaxed setting without interruptions. Retreats also foster mutual trust between the president and the trustees. The agenda should allow ample time for meaningful discussion and should include the following items:

College programs. This provides participants with an overview of the expression of the college mission through its programs. A review of the president's annual report, with time for questions and clarification, is also worthwhile.

Procedures. This activity clarifies role expectations and responsibilities and eliminates duplication of effort. This is the time for trustees to express concerns or support, and to resolve any troublesome issues.

Operational styles. Policies and procedures do not address individual styles or approaches unique to one member or the entire team. Open discussion about operational styles garners understanding and support. Other members of the administrative team can also benefit from this discussion.

Values of the board and the president. This interaction focuses on the compatibility of what the president and board consider important for the college. This is also the time for setting goals, which should be consistent with the vision, mission, and strategic plan for the college.

Vision of the board and the president. The entire leadership team must be involved in vision development to create a sense of ownership and understanding. This is an opportunity for the board to provide direction and support to the president, which is their primary responsibility. The president then works with college staff to develop priorities to achieve the vision. Progress toward vision achievement should be reported annually by the president with opportunities for board feedback.

To Be the Best

Trust is the key to positive and productive board-president relations. Just as each community college is different, so is each president and trustee. Build on the foundation of respect and integrity, find the style that is the most successful for the individuals involved, and adapt. Building trust is not difficult if the board's goal is to be the best it is capable of being. As Terry O'Banion, executive director of the League for Innovation in the Community College, said, "Boards that want to hold on to their presidents must build on a balanced climate in which the board both challenges and supports the president in leading and managing the college. If the board challenges and supports the president to be the best president possible, by that action the board is also becoming the best board they can be" (1989, p. 8).

Together, the trustees and the president form the community college's leadership team. The team members challenge one another to see that every unmet need is filled, every resource wisely invested. To continue the rich tradition they have inherited, each member of the leadership team must find value in mutual support. From the most senior members to the newest members of the team, we must all maintain and enhance the environment that makes the community college the best investment in public education.

The future success of the community college is ensured if the relationship between the board and its president is strong and if the college and its leadership are held in high regard. From this foundation, all else falls into place: enrollments rise, bond issues pass, fund drives are successful, morale is high. The mission is fulfilled. Anything less questions the sincerity of our commitment to public service.

References

American Association of Community Colleges. *Building Communities: A Vision for a New Century.* Washington, D.C.: American Association of Community and Junior Colleges, 1988.

League for Innovation in the Community College. Results of a survey on boards and board relations, March 7, 1996.

O'Banion, T. "Retaining a Peak Performing President." *Trustee Quarterly,* Fall 1989, 7–11.

Vaughan, G. B. Community college presidency turnover study (untitled). Unpublished raw data, 1995.

Vaughan, G. B., and Weisman, I. M. Community college trustee study (untitled). Unpublished raw data, 1995.

Vaughan, G. B., and Weisman, I. M. Community college president study (untitled). Unpublished raw data, 1996.

NORM NIELSEN has been the president of Kirkwood Community College in Cedar Rapids, Iowa, for ten years.

WAYNE NEWTON has been a member of the Kirkwood Community College board of trustees for twenty-three years and has served as chair since 1984.

The seating of new trustees changes the complexion of any board and begins a new set of relationships among board members and between the board and the college president.

When Boards Change: Presidential Response

George R. Boggs, Cindra J. Smith

A governing board is more than the sum of its individual members. Interactions among members and between the college president or district chancellor and the members cause boards to be dynamic and complex entities. Over time, the board and president develop a culture and a way of operating. When the composition of the board changes, new members may bring new ideas and perspectives, but they may also challenge the dominant culture.

To be effective in leading the college district, the president and board must have a clear idea of the roles they are expected to play, and they must work to make the relationship a productive one. Ideally, the president and the board are a team of leaders who share common philosophies and objectives. Because of the visibility of this leadership team, its behavior and effectiveness set the tone for the behavior of others at the college. Clearly, for the college to be successful the president and the board of trustees need to develop and maintain a well-defined, trusting, and effective relationship (Boggs, 1995a).

Those community colleges commonly identified as being among the best have a history of stable presidential leadership (Roueche and Baker, 1987). Long-term presidents attribute their longevity in great degree to the stability of their boards. In these cases, changes in board composition have been gradual enough for new board members to become acculturated and to learn their roles as college trustees. More dramatic changes can challenge a board and president to maintain effective leadership.

In their discussions with presidents, the authors found that presidential turnover often occurs after a large-scale change in board composition. This is especially true if the new members have special interests that they place above the interests of the college, or if they have political ambitions beyond the college board. Boards that are split along philosophical or personal lines have a difficult time providing consistent and effective leadership and can create time-consuming problems for their presidents and their colleges.

Presidential Survey

To learn more about the causes, nature, and consequences of board changes in community college districts, we interviewed eighteen current or retired presidents. In this chapter, the term *president* means college president or district chief administrative officer reporting to a governing board of trustees. This term includes individuals with such titles as chancellor, superintendent/president, and director, as well as president. The interviews were conducted either in person or by telephone from late May to late July 1996. After consulting with recognized community college leaders, we selected presidents who have histories of long service. Collectively, they have served as presidents of thirty different community college districts in ten states. Both multicollege and single college districts were represented, ranging in student enrollment from fifteen hundred to fifty-five thousand. Those presidents interviewed served elected boards as well as appointed boards. One interviewee had experience as a state chancellor.

Board Change

One thing is certain: the composition of a board eventually changes. Board members move from the district. They retire from the board or choose not to seek reelection or reappointment. Some die in office. Others are unseated in elections or are not reappointed by the appointing authority. New board members are chosen to replace those who leave the board.

The motivation for people to serve on community college governing boards is, for the most part, individually derived. Some board members serve because of a sense of civic responsibility or a belief that they should contribute to the well-being of their community. Others serve because they care about the particular college, or education in general. Some board members enjoy the visibility and prestige that comes with college stewardship. Some see board service solely as a step toward another political office, and others may have been elected or appointed to represent special or single interests. In most cases, people who become trustees want to make a difference for their college.

Changes over Time. The presidents whom we interviewed unanimously agreed that the nature of board membership has changed over the years. For the most part, they believed that community college boards have lost many community leaders who served solely because of their interest in public service. One respondent believed that in the past, people felt more obligated to help with the scouts, the church, the schools, or the local community college than is the case today. In his view, communities were smaller and less complex twenty years ago. This same president believed decisions in some states to pay stipends and to grant benefits to board members encouraged a different type of individual to seek appointment or election to community college governing boards.

One respondent reported that the board that hired him included a former state governor, a lawyer, and a doctor. Eventually, those members left and were replaced by members who were less well-known and more concerned with short-term issues and their own special interests. He noted that the latter trustees would vote without pause to spend $10 million but would waste a great deal of time debating details. Another respondent recalled that in the early 1960s five of the ten wealthiest men in the county served on his board. Those trustees would not hesitate to donate $5,000 each to finance a college bond campaign. The respondent thought that this would not happen today.

Other presidents said that people are now more interested in promoting single issues than they were twenty years ago. The presidents noted the transitions from community business leaders serving on boards in earlier times, to people interested in community service, and finally to special-interest-group members. According to a number of presidents interviewed, business leaders seem less inclined to serve on boards today because of the public scrutiny of candidates' personal finances, employee union activities involving picketing and boycotting of those businesses associated with board members, and the necessity of making the unpopular decisions inherent in tough financial times.

The presidents agreed that serving on boards is more difficult today: members have to deal with more conflict, more competition for resources, and more difficult choices. In the past, boards had different issues to deal with; for example, colleges were in their growth years, and boards had more authority and influence.

Only one interviewee believed that boards have improved over the years. In his opinion, thirty years ago boards were rubber stamps for paternalistic presidents or chairs, and not nearly as well informed as they should have been. Today, he sees a higher level of responsibility, with better educated and more knowledgeable trustees studying reports and asking questions. He attributed this change to the need for boards to be involved in effectiveness measures required by today's accreditation standards. The president believed that a downside to boards' being more informed is that trustees may become involved in micromanaging.

Another president stated her belief that boards are more demanding now, and expectations for the board are greater than before. She believed this change has come about because America has ended its love affair with higher education.

Most of the presidents agreed that there is a trend toward micromanaging and not respecting the line between policy and operations. The respondents attributed this to several factors. Changing board membership was identified as a significant factor. In some states, California for instance, local boards have lost authority over the larger issues to state boards and the legislature, leaving boards with fewer policy-level decisions and more time to focus on details. Boards today are under more pressure from state and national bodies to be accountable, and since public resources have declined, trustees spend more time scrutinizing how funds are spent. Board members who feel an obligation or allegiance to employee unions are often pulled into discussions of issues well beyond the policy level. Trustees who want to use the experience as a springboard to another political office may try to build a résumé of personal accomplishments, often focusing on administrative rather than policy-level issues.

Although the nature of boards may have changed over time, each individual change can be significant for a board-president team. With even one change, the chemistry of the board is altered. For the most part, interviewees indicated that a president can help prevent disruption when a board changes. In fact, two of the respondents felt that presidents deserved the boards they have, implying that a president can shape the character of the board.

Board Candidates

The responses of the presidents were mixed when asked about their identifying candidates for their boards and becoming involved in the appointment or election process. Most of those interviewed felt that presidents should not recruit candidates for board membership, and most have not, despite having had many opportunities. An exception to this rule, according to one respondent, arises when a declared candidate wants to replace the president, in which case the president has little to lose by backing someone else. Some presidents have also been involved in identifying candidates for appointment or encouraging good people to run or seek appointment when an incumbent is not seeking reelection or reappointment.

Some respondents encouraged their trustees to identify and support candidates who would be good board members. Other presidents talked to their trustees about potential candidates; one was asked by her board chair to suggest a good candidate. In so doing, she considered candidates who would bring racial, gender, and occupational diversity to the board.

One president described a formal board appointment process in which the president is permitted to nominate candidates for consideration by the governor. In addition, he and another president reported having occasional personal contacts with governors about appointments. The contacts were sometimes initiated by the presidents, at other times by the governors. In the 1960s, when one respondent's board was more politically influential than today, members would essentially tell the governor whom to appoint. In another state, a president told of a nonpartisan citizens' group being formed some years ago to suggest board members after the college suffered from a lot of controversy and nearly lost its accreditation. This citizens' group now both recommends a slate of candidates for election to the board and finances election campaigns.

Several respondents participated in orientation for prospective board candidates. Some presidents invited candidates to meet for an informal discussion of the college and board responsibilities; others conducted a structured orientation session. The orientation sessions were designed to answer the candidates' questions and to supply information about the college and the board. Candidates must be ensured equal opportunity. Presidents believed the more information given to candidates about the roles of board members, the better. Board candidate forums, on the other hand, are best organized without the direct involvement of the president, although it is probably a good idea for the president to attend these forums (Boggs, 1995a).

Challenges of Change

Change is always difficult; even when a board and president have developed a trusting, effective, professional relationship, change in board membership may be perceived as a threat to a comfortable organizational culture. Certain circumstances, however, may make the change even more difficult for the board and the president, as well as for the college community. The circumstances identified by the respondents include changes that bring special interests to the board, those that result in a split board, those that bring renegade trustees to the board, and those that present the president with moral or ethical dilemmas. Some of the challenges caused by these circumstances were significant enough to cause presidential turnover.

Special Interests. According to Axelrod (1989), the tradition of governance by qualified lay people unencumbered by special interests is basic to the philosophy of higher education in America. Other authorities agree that trustees have an obligation to remain independent of special interests or groups (Ingram, 1988). Every person has special interests, however. Most people belong to groups that advocate certain values, ideals, or political or religious beliefs. Unfortunately, these special interests have become single interests among candidates for many public offices today, and because of the passion involved, candidates with special interests are not easy to deal with. When a trustee or a president places a special interest ahead of the best interests of the college, the college suffers, and the jobs of the president and the rest of the board members become more difficult.

Board members should rise above their own individual interests to consider the diversity of values, philosophies, needs, and wants in the community. They are responsible for seeking input from all "owners" of the college in order to identify the common good and act in the best interests of the college (Carver, 1993). Unfortunately, this does not always happen.

In one case, a president was directed by his board to remove the college's financial accounts from a bank with whom they did business because of its donations to an organization accused of discrimination against homosexuals. In this case, a newly elected board member with a special interest in gay rights was able to convince other trustees to support his cause.

Several presidents had members elected to the board with an agenda of diverting college business to firms owned and operated by minorities and women. While it can be argued that this issue makes the college more socially conscious, time spent debating the matter diverts personnel from issues that may be more central to the college mission. Moreover, the line between special interest and conflict of interest is in fact sometimes crossed. Respondents have had to deal with trustees who wanted business to go to friends and relatives or wanted college jobs for them.

One president related concerns about the growing strength of the "religious right" in board elections. Because of the very active involvement of churches in some areas of the country, candidates supported by the religious right have unseated incumbents. The potential exists for these boards to be diverted from college policy issues to those involving abortion, sex education, evolution, creationism, and other issues of religious concern.

Board members elected with the support of employee unions may also have a biased view of their responsibilities. In some instances, presidents have observed board members going to dinner with employee union presidents just prior to board meetings. Some of the presidents thought these trustees believed they represented employees rather than the community.

Split Boards. Some presidents have had to deal with boards that were consistently split along philosophical, racial, or personal lines. These split boards are not only very difficult for trustees and presidents but also very disruptive for a college district. One respondent experienced five changes in board chairs involving only two people during his tenure with one community college district. The board was divided along racial lines, and each board election changed the racial balance of the board. Another respondent reported a board split philosophically as to whether it should increase taxes in order to accommodate a larger enrollment with greater diversity of students.

The president and board should not view lack of consensus as a weakness. Board members bring a variety of perspectives to their roles. It may not always be possible for the board, even after thorough discussion, to reach consensus on every issue. In such cases, the president should help all board members respect the minority opinion while supporting the decision of the majority. The board and the president must move on to the next issue without being influenced by hard feelings from a previous decision (Boggs, 1995b).

One respondent dealt with a board conflict in which a trustee supported an unsuccessful candidate for appointment to the board and then had difficulty working with the candidate who was appointed. Another president reported that he eventually left his position with a college because he could not get the board to overcome internal differences and work together.

In the case of appointed boards, presidents described a trend toward political patronage. Rather than seeking candidates who might be best for the board, appointing bodies sometimes view board appointments as rewards. This can be especially disruptive if appointments are made along party lines, resulting in a board that is likewise split. In one instance, appointees of a new governor were recipients of political patronage, and the president was not able to orient them to their role as policy makers. Members of the board who had been appointed by the previous governor and who were concerned about policy eventually resigned rather than deal with the philosophical split and the new board members' interest in detail.

Renegade Trustees. Renegade board members are defined as those trustees who are not willing to work with the rest of the board as a team or who work against the board or the president. These renegades may or may not have a single agenda. They present themselves as individualistic and independent, and they are unlikely to work with other board members and the president as a team. They might not respect the confidentiality of closed or executive sessions. They tend to suspect conspiracies and sometimes independently leak issues to the press or even take legal action against the college district.

Moral and Ethical Dilemmas. Several presidents have faced moral or ethical dilemmas after a change in board composition. One president reported that he was summoned to a meeting in the board chair's office on a Saturday morning. Another trustee joined them, and the two handed the president a list of administrators they wanted fired. On another occasion, this same president was told by members of the board to back off on the findings of an audit.

Some trustees want friends or relatives hired or enemies fired. In other cases, trustees have asked that contracts be awarded to family members, friends, or supporters. Each of these circumstances presents a dilemma for a president who serves a board and is trying to make it work as a team. The president must hold firm to fundamental principles of business ethics.

When Changes Cause Presidential Turnover

Working with special-interest trustees, split boards that refuse to work as a unit, and renegade trustees, as well as being asked to violate ethical principles are reasons cited by presidents for leaving a position. One respondent said that the president is the ultimate scapegoat: if he or she cannot make the board work, the president eventually gets the blame and frequently is the one to leave.

Two presidents left their positions when their boards became deadlocked by opposing factions and it was unlikely that the presidents' contracts would be renewed. Another president resigned because a board chair had been appointed by the governor over the objections of the president. Still another president's contract was renewed even though board members had been appointed with the intent to get rid of him. Later, he was able to leave on his own terms.

One president said he could have stayed in his position, but he could not get the board to work together, and so when another opportunity arose he took it. Another president retired a year earlier than he had planned because he was not enjoying his job as much as in the past. His previous boards had been a pleasure to work with, but trying to work with the new board took the enjoyment from his job.

The beginning of the end for one president occurred when the board turned down his recommendation for vice president, appointing someone else to the vice presidency for political reasons. The board differed from the president on other issues as well and even met without the president being present.

Strategies for Success

Although some of the presidents in the sample were faced with untenable situations and eventually left their positions, others successfully negotiated the challenges of board changes. All of the presidents surveyed were experienced presidents, and they shared their strategies for success. The strategies include board orientation and development, evaluation of the president and the board, developing a long-term perspective, and working with effective board chairs.

Board Orientation. All of the respondents reported conducting formal orientations with new board members, and all felt these sessions were valuable. The orientation sessions provided an opportunity for the president and college staff to inform the new trustees about the college, its mission, and its operations while providing an opportunity for the new trustees to learn more about their role in policy setting and monitoring. Often the board chair or an experienced trustee helped with the orientation. Sometimes a consultant from a state or national trustee organization served as a facilitator. Written materials about the college, board responsibilities, and board ethics were commonly distributed and reviewed.

Other interviewees conducted informal orientation sessions, often during a campus tour. According to the respondents, informal settings provided an excellent opportunity for the president to explain important issues and to introduce the new board member to faculty and staff. One-on-one informal meetings enabled the new trustee to ask questions that might be difficult to raise in a more formal setting. One respondent said a president should spend as much time as possible one-on-one with new trustees. Another noted that it takes up to two years for a new trustee to become fully oriented to the position.

Respondents also talked of the value of orientation sessions scheduled by state trustee associations. The presidents all encouraged new trustees to attend sessions where policy-making responsibilities, legal requirements, and open meeting laws are discussed with trustees. Trustees are reminded in these sessions that they have no authority as an individual.

One respondent said that new trustees will be oriented by somebody, and it had better be the president. In a survey of local board orientation practices, the president was identified by board chairs, new trustees, and presidents as the most important contributor (Smith, 1995). Even trustees who were elected with a special-interest agenda sometimes began to change their perspectives as a result of well-organized formal and informal orientation sessions.

Board Communication and Development. The education and development of board members should not stop after an initial orientation. Presidents who have successfully met the challenges of board changes stated that establishing and maintaining healthy board relations is a primary responsibility of the president and that regular and ongoing communication is a key factor in success. These presidents always kept their trustees informed, sent them information regularly, met with them individually over breakfast or lunch, and called them frequently. The presidents spent the time necessary to address trustee concerns, answer their questions, and move them toward a common mission and direction. Telephone messages from board members were among the very first to which the presidents responded. Presidents considered it perhaps even more important to spend time with trustees they do not like or who are not supportive of them. Respondents who have done this were sometimes able to turn negative trustees into supporters.

Presidents also supported the trustee education programs sponsored by state and national trustee associations and encouraged their board members to attend trustee conferences. Another strategy used by presidents is to help trustees develop a sense of pride in their community colleges and their service as board members. Presidents should point out significant issues for trustees to address that both meet their needs and further the goals of the institution. Presidents can capitalize on a new trustee's desire to make a difference.

The respondents also considered board workshops very valuable. With such problems as a split board, overriding special interests, or renegade board members, a workshop with an outside facilitator can help the group become a cohesive team. No one should expect one workshop to solve serious board problems, however. What can result is a plan for building a better board. Even in cases where there are no serious problems on a board, occasional workshops, study sessions, or retreats are valuable in maintaining a leadership team focused on the best interests of the college.

Long-Range Focus. Another strategy used by the respondents is to focus the board on strategic issues. The magnitude of challenges facing colleges requires that boards encourage positive institutional response to societal changes. Board agendas and workshops should include discussion of substantive educational and organizational issues, not just business items. For example, substantive discussions between the board members and college staff on meaningful long-term issues should be encouraged. Presidents can play a major role in structuring board agendas so that their boards discuss larger issues of institutional direction and effectiveness rather than operational details. Ensuring that board members are educated about important issues facing the college elevates their role and expands their perspectives. Involving the board in discussions about future issues and plans is essential.

One respondent who dealt with a renegade trustee elected with support from a special-interest group was successful in getting the board to function together because she moved them toward long-range planning, the development of a vision for the future of the college district, and the preparation of related goals and objectives. This president consciously chose not to place on the board agenda issues that would ignite controversy.

Expectations and Evaluation. Regular evaluations of presidential and board performance provide opportunities for the board and the president to clarify expectations and assess progress toward meeting college or district goals. Kerr and Gade (1989) went so far as to say that boards should realize that, when they evaluate their president, they are also evaluating their own performance. Many districts, however, separate board and presidential evaluations.

In any case, it is essential for the president to know what the board expects and that the criteria for evaluation reflect the aggregate interests and values of the board (Carver and Mayhew, 1994). Groharing (1991) identified lack of agreement on expectations between the board and president as a major reason for a high turnover of presidents in Illinois community colleges.

As new members come onto a board, it is important to review what the goals of the college are and what is expected of the president. Those presidents who were interviewed who successfully dealt with board change made annual objectives the basis for their evaluation. The presidents discussed these objectives with new trustees shortly after they joined the board. Most of our interviewees stated that the president should always take the lead in developing a draft of presidential objectives for board review. These objectives should be related to the long-range plan and vision of the district and should be compatible with the mission.

The President-Board Chair Partnership. An effective board chair can be most helpful when there are problems with a board member. Popcock points out that no president should be expected to discipline a board member (1988). When there is a problem with a board member, a board chair or another influential board member can be very helpful in discussing concerns with the particular trustee in private. There may be occasions in which the whole board may have to deal with a disruptive trustee or with one who is not living up to the board's expectations or standards of ethics. Like it or not, open-meeting laws in some states do not permit the board to address these issues in closed or executive sessions.

One respondent indicated that her board chair conducts the annual board evaluation by reviewing goal accomplishments and questioning the other members about board accomplishments. Another president went to his board chair for help when a trustee asked him to do something which he, the president, believed to be unethical.

In some community college districts, the board chair rotates annually. In others, the chair is elected by members of the board, and a particular trustee may remain in the chair position for several years. One of the respondents preferred a rotating chair because it diminishes the authority of the chair with respect to the president. However, in other cases presidents preferred strong board chairs who could help orient new trustees and help the president deal with problems on the board.

Recommendations

The respondents who were interviewed have many years of experience in dealing with board change. In some cases, the presidents were able to conclude long and successful careers in a district, working to acculturate new trustees as they were seated. In other cases, presidents could not bring a board together and retired early or left for new positions. All of the respondents provided words of advice, and some commented on things they would do differently if they had a chance.

Most presidents emphasize the need to establish a positive relationship with new trustees. Once established, this relationship must be cultivated and maintained. Although these activities take time away from other leadership responsibilities, the presidents consider it time well spent. Successful presidents keep an ear to the ground to sense potential problems before they develop and then work to resolve them before they become serious. Continuous communication between the president and the individual trustees is also important. Complete honesty is seen as critical, and all agree that trustees should be protected from surprises. Respect for individual differences and perspectives is also identified as a key to good relations.

Respondents who have confronted moral and ethical dilemmas advise that a president should never compromise his or her principles. A leader's integrity should not yield to pressure. One respondent said that presidents should know their own values and decide where to draw the limits, using common sense in gray areas. Presidents should always have sufficient resources and enough courage to leave a position when staying would cost them their personal integrity.

One respondent, who was faced with five new members on a seven-member board, took too much responsibility upon himself for trying to orient the board. He would now recommend involving the remaining experienced board members and his senior administrators in helping the board work as a team and focus on policy issues.

If they had it to do over again, two respondents would use more tact in dealing with board members, especially in open meetings. These presidents would find a different way of communicating their disagreement with board members.

Another respondent advises presidents to protect themselves by negotiating separation clauses and early retirement benefits into employment contracts. Yet another encourages presidents to call on their own political support early enough to make a difference in dealing with changes on the board. Other presidents discuss methods of coping with challenges, including keeping physically fit, living a balanced life, being future-oriented, and maintaining integrity. Others seek support from spouses, their cabinets, other presidents, consultants who work with presidents, and therapists.

Conclusion

Board changes, like presidential changes, bring a new complexion to the leadership of a community college district. If the change is gradual and the new trustee understands the policy-making role of the board and does not have a special interest unaligned with the mission and goals of the district, the change can be a healthy one. On the other hand, change often presents challenges. Presidents and boards can benefit from the experience of other presidents who have faced these kinds of changes. Community colleges require the effective leadership of dedicated and informed teams of trustees and presidents.

References

Axelrod, N. R. *A Guide for New Trustees*. Washington, D.C.: Association of Governing Boards of Universities and Colleges, 1989.

Boggs, G. R. "The President and the Board." In G. A. Baker III and Associates (eds.), *Team Building for Quality: Transitions in the American Community College*. Washington, D.C.: The American Association of Community Colleges, 1995a.

Boggs, G. R. "Matching CEO and Board Expectations." *Trustee Quarterly,* 1995b, Issue 4, 8–14.

Carver, J. "Achieving Meaningful Diversity in the Board Room." *Board Leadership,* July-Aug. 1993, *8* (1), 4–5.

Carver, J., and Mayhew, M. *A New Vision of Board Leadership: Governing in the Community Colleges*. Washington, D.C.: Association of Community College Trustees, 1994.

Groharing, R. "A Primer on Board/CEO Relations." *Illinois Trustee,* Apr.-May 1991, 8–10.

Ingram, R. T. "Organizing the Board." In R. T. Ingram and Associates (eds.), *Making Trusteeship Work*. Washington, D.C.: Association of Governing Boards of Universities and Colleges, 1988.

Kerr, C., and Gade, M. *The Guardians: Boards of Trustees of American Colleges and Universities*. Washington, D.C.: Association of Governing Boards of Universities and Colleges, 1989.

Popcock, J. W. "Maintaining Effective Chair-CEO Relationships." In R. T. Ingram and Associates, *Making Trusteeship Work*. Washington, D.C.: Association of Governing Boards of Universities and Colleges, 1988.

Roueche, J. E., and Baker, G. A., III. *Access and Excellence: The Open-Door College*. Washington, D.C.: American Association of Community Colleges, 1987.

Smith, C. J. *Local Trustee Orientation Programs*. Sacramento: Community College League of California, 1995.

GEORGE R. BOGGS *is superintendent/president of Palomar College in San Marcos, California, and past chair of the board of directors of the American Association of Community Colleges.*

CINDRA J. SMITH *is director of education services for the Community College League of California in Sacramento.*

Today, change is the rule, not the exception. In order to deal
successfully with change, community college boards must
become cohesive, effective teams.

Opportunities and Challenges
for Boards in Times of Change

Montez C. Martin, Jr.

Change is the single most salient characteristic of community college boards
in the last two decades. We've been a movement in a hurry! During the 1960s
and 1970s, many trustees were long-term servants of their college, elected or
appointed by throwing their hats into the ring or by being drafted by public
officials. Increasingly, however, during the 1980s and 1990s, community colleges have become more visible and more appreciated, and trusteeship has
become a more desirable position. Consequently, whether board members are
elected or appointed, typically there are several well-qualified candidates for
each board position. This stiffer competition may result in stronger candidates;
it certainly results in greater change. On the governing board of Trident Technical College (TTC) in Charleston, South Carolina, every board member I
served with in 1982 has retired, passed away, or been replaced. Concurrent
with the turnover in board membership, there have been five changes in the
board chair, and the college has had four presidents and two interim presidents
in those fourteen years. To afford opportunity for leadership, we trustees at
TTC modified our bylaws in the early 1990s to limit board chairmanship to
two terms, thereby ensuring change in the chair's position.

Since the establishment of the college in 1963, TTC has had eleven actual
or interim presidents. This rate of a new president every three years exceeds
the average seven-year tenure of most community college presidents. Thus,
my fourteen years of board experience have reinforced the necessity of
acknowledging two simple maxims. First, change is the rule, not the exception. We must make change positive, not negative; evolutionary, not revolutionary. And second, the board has to make itself into an effective
team—immediately and continuously.

Eliminating Negative Consequences of Change

Since change is the rule, early recognition and appreciation of the leadership roles and communication styles of each board member are critical to the effectiveness of the board. There are at least three types of leadership roles on each board: official leaders, as established by the bylaws; emotional leaders, as determined by the passion and communication skills of the individual; and situational leaders, as determined by the expertise of individual members. Taking these attributes into account helps in developing rapport among the board. Obviously, personal and professional rapport is important for board effectiveness, especially as changes occur in board membership.

Boards need to work continuously to establish and foster respect and rapport among the board members. Time constraints make this difficult during regular meetings. This is one reason why boards should have annual retreats. In addition to substantive sessions, retreats should include time for trustees to get to know each other informally. We need to understand each other's interests and concerns. We need to recognize that we do not all approach issues and problems in the same manner. We need to recognize and appreciate our diversity—whether it is by race, gender, age, or political affiliation. We can make these differences positive factors for the college if we take advantage of our differences and our individual links to various segments of the community.

In one of my very first board meetings at Trident, we were wrestling with the problem of trying to relocate our downtown campus from a school building we had leased from the county school district. The district wanted the building back. So we faced several questions regarding change of location: Where should we locate the campus? How much should we pay? Should we lease or buy? Which terms would be negotiable, and which wouldn't be? We were able to take advantage of several board members' backgrounds: a developer, a real estate broker, an engineer, a school administrator, and a social worker all brought specialized expertise to the table. The developer and real estate broker had obvious experience in site selection and contract negotiations. The engineer provided valuable assistance in evaluating the condition of the building. Because the site was an abandoned high school, the school administrator was able to assist in understanding the internal operations and politics of the school district. The social worker took the lead in developing the communication plan for informing the surrounding neighbors of our intentions. She also worked with the faculty and staff to understand this inner-city neighborhood and its unique history and needs.

A split vote of five to four on purchasing the abandoned high school inflicted some wounds, but the board was able to heal them by pulling together as a team and communicating regularly and frequently. Although we were anxious and concerned about our decision, it has since been vindicated by the success of Palmer Campus, which has experienced a 128 percent enrollment increase to over fifteen hundred students since we opened the doors in 1986.

Establishing procedures and processes proactively is crucial to the efficiency and smooth functioning of the board. Here are a few suggestions to reduce the negative aspects of inevitable changes in board membership:

- Review the college's bylaws, mission, and other official documents regularly.
- Review board meeting minutes to ensure completeness and accuracy.
- Adopt parliamentary procedures before there is a problem or conflict.
- Establish a conflict resolution process before it is needed.
- Adopt a governing model that can absorb board changes and controversy.
- Acknowledge that since colleges are academic institutions, a collegiate decision-making model is best. Deliberation and intellectual challenges should be welcomed.

By adopting these preventive measures, the board should be able to absorb and adapt to new members, including those with strong personal or political agendas. The response to change can then be positive and evolutionary, not negative and revolutionary.

The board's duty is to provide insight and oversight for the college administration. We trustees cannot simply represent a specific constituency or special interest. Our responsibility is to the whole college.

As trustees, we cannot allow ourselves to be seduced by the comfort and simplicity of making day-to-day operational decisions. Those decisions are easier to make, but they are not the board's responsibility. We need to remind ourselves at every meeting that our responsibility is to look at the big picture and major policies. We do not need to meddle in management responsibilities, however tempting that might be.

When I think about my responsibility as a board member, I always keep the president's perspective in the back of my mind. Yet, I realize that our board has not always functioned to allow the president to be as effective as possible. For instance, one of our presidents resigned shortly before I joined the board. We behaved in a fairly normal—but reactionary—mode: we told the new president everything that had led to his predecessor's departure. We also gave him an extensive list of things he could not do. One such edict was that he could not travel out of the community without advance approval of the board—not even to a meeting of the presidents of the state's sixteen technical colleges. Looking back, I wonder how and why he survived our meddling. Under such circumstances, we could have done great and lasting damage to the college. Change, especially change sparked by negative publicity and mismanagement, sometimes brings on this type of overbearing micromanagement. It should not. Boards must resist the temptation to micromanage in times of change. We must do what we can to have processes and procedures in place to thwart our tendency to "fight the last war."

Forming the Effective Team

Establishing Context. Context is the key for creating the effective board. Just as a verse of scripture must be placed in context for clarity and completeness, so must the work of the board be placed in a larger context for understanding.

Establishment of this context begins early for new board members, with an orientation that is exemplary and not perfunctory. The orientation should be provided by two "master teachers": the president and the board chair. Whereas the context of board service is skillfully established through trustee orientation, it is enhanced through continuing education. Historically, community colleges have preached the imperative of lifelong learning. We as trustees now must practice what we preach, promoting lifelong learning throughout the trustee's life on the board. Naturally, as the chair of the Association of Community College Trustees board of directors, I believe that professional development through ACCT conferences and seminars is an excellent way to continue "lifelong learning" for board members.

Role of the Community College. To really understand the role of the community college board member, the trustee must first understand the history of the community college. Unlike national or regional institutions, community colleges belong to their local service areas. Woven into the very fabric of the community it serves, a community college must be responsive and accessible. Typically, it is open door. Through that door walk remedial students, vocational students, college transfer students, and workers needing occupational upgrading. These students are diverse and overwhelmingly part-time. Meeting such varied needs is, of course, a challenge. Acknowledging the challenge, Bell observes that "community colleges almost defy the time-honored phrase that you can't be all things to all people. These remarkable institutions come closer to it than any other college in the world of academe. They are flexible, adaptive, and open. They are close to their students and sensitive to their students' needs" (1993, p. 8).

It is essential that trustees study and understand the history and role of the community college. The initial orientation of the board members should include significant information on the history and role of the community college.

Maintaining Unity Amid Change

It is critical that the board maintain unity in public. A divided board is not as effective as it needs to be—agree to disagree, and move on to the next issue. Otherwise, you could hinder the effectiveness of the college, the morale of the faculty and staff, and the ability to obtain the public and private financial support critical to the college's very existence.

Currently, I am fortunate to be a part of a community college board whose members understand and practice the rule that the board should act only as a whole. Individual board members have no authority to act unilaterally, and individuals do not speak for the board unless authorized to do so.

Of course, there are times when the board makes a decision that you, as a trustee, disagree with and vote against. Publicly, you should defend the decision, or at least remain silent. If the issue is sufficiently important and if you cannot in conscience agree with the decision publicly, you may have no recourse but to resign from the board.

When our board was wrestling with the decision to relocate the TTC downtown campus, the final vote to acquire the property was five to four. I am proud of how we overcame our differences through teamwork. We disagreed, sometimes vehemently, before the vote, but we always provided the public with a united front. Although the Palmer Campus became a successful reality, it did so at the expense of losing one of our longest-serving and most dedicated board members. He voted against the project, yet he supported the board's decision to proceed, and then he worked to make it a success. However, late into the development of the campus, he came to a difficult decision. He told the board of his love for the college and the inner turmoil he had suffered as a result of the board's decision to purchase the chosen property. He concluded that it was time to resign from the board. Although we respected his decision, we regretted losing him as a fellow board member.

Role of the Chair in Helping the Board Cope with Change

The chair has to play several roles, often more than one at a time. John W. Nason describes the chairman's responsibility well in *The Nature of Trusteeship: The Role and Responsibilities of College and University Boards*: "The chairman must moderate as well as lead—a healer of breaches, harmonizer of divisiveness, sometimes cajoler and, when necessary, a disciplinarian. To the public the chairman is the symbol of the board and very often its spokesman. Within the board the chairman sets the example for the other trustees by his or her personal performance" (1982, p. 83).

It is this last point—setting the example—that in the end is probably the most important. In my first full year as chair of the board at TTC, I participated in my third presidential search as a board member. The board that chose the new president was comprised of eight men and one woman, the latter having joined the board in the last month of the presidential search. Our hiring Mary Thornley, the first woman president at Trident, provided opportunities and challenges for the board and for me as chair.

The first of those challenges came as we narrowed the search to five finalists. Then the board was fully informed of the gender and ethnicity of the finalists. As board members, we all had to set aside stereotypes and our own preconceived notions. This was the first time an African American or a woman had been included as a finalist in any presidential search at Trident. I was very pleased that the board could deliberate so effectively as a team to determine which of those well-qualified candidates would best serve Trident. It was gratifying to see the immediate recognition of the opportunities that lay ahead and that the selection process, though daunting, was a success.

Evolving Missions Reflect Change over Time

The responsibility of the board includes establishing policy, which of course includes establishing the college's mission. At the core of board effectiveness is its grasp of the institution's mission. An example of an evolving mission is found in the history of Trident Technical College.

When TTC opened its doors in 1964, it was part of a statewide system of sixteen technical colleges designed to meet the training needs of South Carolina business and industry and to offer credit programs in industrial and engineering technology. That original purpose has been retained, but it has become one part of a greatly expanded mission. In 1973, the college merged with a junior college that offered business and parallel programs; subsequently TTC added these programs to its list of approved curricula. In the late 1970s, when the Medical University of South Carolina ended programs at the associate degree level, Trident Technical College began offering a variety of health programs.

Responding to identified local needs, the college next added hospitality and tourism, criminal justice, and legal assistant programs. In short, during its thirty-three-year history, Trident has evolved into a comprehensive two-year college. In that time, credit enrollment catapulted from 224 students in 1964 to 9,500 in 1996.

Although the college is comprehensive, the word *technical* has been deliberately retained in the name to harken back to its original purpose and to state clearly the direct link to economic development. Like many colleges, Trident's mission has evolved from narrow to comprehensive. I have provided the history of Trident as an example of how and why a college can evolve over time. Such evolutions warrant careful explanation and establishment of context. Only then can board members respond effectively to concerns from the public about the college remaining true to its mission.

It merits attention that *mission*, a term from Latin, is often used in religious contexts. Like any zealous missionary, board members should likewise commit to the college's mission. In order to be effective missionaries, we have to know our past, be alert in the present, and dream big dreams for the future.

Forming the Effective Board-Team:
Trident's Quality Management

A recognized challenge for all college boards is to form a cohesive, effective team. Reflecting on my own four years (two terms) as board chair of Trident Technical College, I am convinced that TTC's approach to creating process-improvement teams is a sensible, worthwhile step toward developing a cohesive, effective team of board members.

This idea was driven home to us by President Thornley one day in August 1992 at the fall collegewide meeting. That day, she introduced the concepts of continuous-improvement teams and quality initiatives to all of the college's five hundred employees. She shared her compelling reasons for initiating a quality approach at TTC. They were personal, practical, and financial; they reflected no federal, state, or local mandate, nor one from our governing board. Since that date, the college has made great strides toward being quality-driven. Eleven different process improvement teams (PITs), comprised of employees from across the college, have tackled such processes as the hiring of perma-

nent employees and the purchase of college library books. While this trans-
formation has not been driven by the governing board, trustees have been ben-
eficiaries of the college's successes in developing teams.

President Thornley first introduced the board to these concepts at the
1992 board retreat. She then continued to reinforce this philosophy and
approach at every board retreat and in regular reports to the board. I think we
finally got it. We have recognized the transferability of the team concepts to
effective trusteeship.

For the most part, the following characteristics of successful teams also
describe successful boards. The list is a composite from several sources and
was developed by the college for its PIT manual:

- The mission and goals of the team are clearly stated.
- The roles and responsibilities of individual team members are clearly stated.
- Regular meetings are scheduled and meeting times published.
- The team's process for arriving at decisions is clearly stated.
- Methods for obtaining feedback from customers are determined and used.
- Desirable communication practices are defined and then practiced.
- Data gathering is conducted using appropriate methodology and tools.
- The organization's definition and degree of empowerment is clearly stated.
- The team builds in an assessment component of its own activity.

The continuous-improvement process developed within TTC can be coupled with the policy governance model developed by John Carver. His model
allows boards to provide meaningful policy development, outreach to constituencies, and an appropriate relationship with and evaluation of the president. Carver and Mayhew (1990) state that "policy is an apt and familiar
word for us to employ when referring to organizational values and perspectives, but the strength of familiarity is also a weakness. Policies are not
detailed and event-specific governance" (p. 26). Those authors describe four
categories of policy:

1. Ends: the needs the organization intends to meet, and at what cost
2. Executive limitations: the principles of ethics and prudence within which
   the staff exercises its practices and methods
3. Board-executive relationship: delegation to and assessment of the CEO
4. Board process: board procedures and leadership (adapted from Carver
   and Mayhew, 1990)

A board utilizing the Carver model agrees to a disciplined practice of not
interfering with the staff's choices of means used to accomplish the ends. The
board functions effectively in a college that embraces staff empowerment, continuous-improvement processes, and other accountability and institutional-
effectiveness measures. Use of the Carver model promotes accountability at the
college's highest level of decision making.

Also promoting accountability at that highest level are the recommendations of the 1988 report of the Commission on the Future of Community Colleges, *Building Communities: A Vision for a New Century*:

> We recommend that the role of the community college trustees be strengthened. Specifically, the governing board should focus on selecting an effective leader and defining institutional goals. The board also should receive, periodically, sufficient information to know that the college's goals are being met. Trustees should not try to manage the institution.
>
> The education of community college trustees should be expanded. We strongly urge that new trustees participate in an orientation program as a condition of assuming office. We also recommend that they participate in continuing trustee education at local, regional, and national meetings.
>
> The role of the board of trustees and that of the internal governance functions should not be confused. Since trustees are the ultimate authority to which the college is accountable, we recommend that faculty, staff, and student representatives not be appointed or elected to such boards as voting members [Commission on the Future of Community Colleges, 1988, p. 44].

If boards follow these "doctor's orders," coupled with a strong dose of quality-driven continuous improvement, we would have stronger, healthier colleges. Just as business and industry have recognized the necessity of becoming quality driven and team oriented, so must we.

Finally, the goal for effective and cohesive boards is perhaps best captured by Max De Pree in *Leadership Is an Art,* a book written by the chief executive officer of a quality-driven furniture company: "We would like to find the most effective, most productive, most rewarding way of working together. We would like to know that our work process uses all the appropriate and pertinent resources: human, physical, financial. We would like a work process and relationships that meet our personal needs for belonging, for contributing, for meaningful work, for the opportunity to make a commitment, for the opportunity to grow and be at least reasonably in control of our own destinies. Finally, we'd like someone to say 'thank you'" (1989, p. 21).

References

Bell, T. H. "The Role and Future of Community Colleges in America." *School and College,* 1993, 32 (11), 8.

Carver, J., and Mayhew, M. *Boards That Make a Difference.* San Francisco: Jossey-Bass, 1990.

Commission on the Future of Community Colleges. *Building Communities: A Vision for a New Century.* Washington, D.C.: American Association of Community and Junior Colleges, 1988.

De Pree, M. *Leadership Is an Art.* New York: Doubleday, 1989.

Nason, J. W. *The Nature of Trusteeship: The Role and Responsibilities of College and University Boards.* Washington, D.C.: Association of Governing Boards of Universities and Colleges, 1982.

MONTEZ C. MARTIN, JR., *is a trustee at Trident Technical College, Charleston, South Carolina, and chair of the Association of Community College Trustees board of directors.*

A crisis on campus requires that the president and the board of trustees work together to resolve the issue in the best interests of the institution. Resolution is predicated, in large measure, upon the communication skills of the president.

When a Crisis Occurs: A President's Perspective

Sean A. Fanelli

During the fifteen years I have served as president of Nassau Community College (NCC) in Garden City, New York, I have come to know that no institution, no matter its magnitude or environment, is protected from the possibility of an untoward event. What is also clear to me is that crises can take many forms. Whether it is a labor dispute, student disruption on campus, personal tragedy, fire, theft, sexual assault, financial malfeasance, community furor over a speaker or an event, unanticipated downturn in enrollment, reduction in funding, or reduction in force, a board expects the president to demonstrate the leadership and managerial skills necessary to deal effectively with these problems and to avoid or else minimize harm to the institution.

Crises can be likened to natural disasters: some are predictable, others are totally unpredictable. Those we see coming are like hurricanes, for which there is usually ample warning and time to prepare a response; others are like earthquakes, providing little or no warning. In reality, events that presidents and boards deal with lie on a broad continuum between the unforeseen and the foreseen.

Good communication is indispensable and essential for dealing with both types of crises. Based upon my experiences at Nassau, the following practices have proven to be successful in meeting the challenges of these crises. What I have learned simply reinforces the value of good president-board interchange and underscores the peril of incomplete communication.

An open and harmonious relationship between the president and the board of trustees is essential for effective leadership in the collegiate setting. Although there are many circumstances that can strain this relationship, it is at greatest risk during a crisis, external or internal, predictable or unpredictable.

NEW DIRECTIONS FOR COMMUNITY COLLEGES, no. 98, Summer 1997 © Jossey-Bass Publishers

The potential for stress, however, can be reduced and even eliminated if the president takes proper steps before and during a crisis.

The time to prepare for a crisis is *before* one occurs. In an atmosphere free of anxiety and confusion, the board, with the guidance and support of the president, is able to develop procedures for dealing with crises. With procedures already in place, the timely actions of a president can minimize the impact of a crisis upon the president-board relationship; such actions may even lead to a stronger relationship between them. If a crisis is dealt with properly, positive effects can accrue to an institution. In addition, the relationship between the board and president may be strengthened as a result of meeting and overcoming a shared challenge. These results, however, are secondary to the president's first priority in any crisis: to work with the board to resolve the issue at hand and ensure the well-being of the institution.

Examples of Crisis

Nassau Community College is the largest of the thirty community colleges in the State University of New York system. It is a single-campus, suburban college located fifteen miles east of New York City. There are twenty-three thousand students registered in credit courses and approximately fifteen thousand enrolled in credit-free programs. The college has 630 full-time and about 500 part-time faculty, who are represented by two separate and unrelated unions. The college has benefitted from an excellent system of governance. The academic senate is separated from the two faculty unions; its membership is comprised of faculty, administrators, and students.

The college has an autonomous ten-person board of trustees whose members are appointed for nine-year terms. Five trustees are appointed by the local county sponsor, four are appointed by the governor, and one student trustee (with full voting rights) is elected by the students each academic year. Typically, one appointed board member and the student trustee are replaced on the board each year. This statutorily mandated arrangement has the distinct benefit of providing both continuity and change on the board.

During my presidency, NCC has sustained attacks on academic freedom. The first was brought on as some individuals in the community deemed irreverent a play presented by the college theater department. The second attack came from citizens objecting to the contents of a human sexuality course. In both instances, the board reached consensus and took decisive action to uphold academic freedom. The board was firm in its resolve not to allow the curriculum to be dictated by those external to the college's process of governance. These issues drew national attention, including coverage on CNN's "Larry King Live" show.

Labor relations have created some crises. Although relations with the union representing full-time faculty at NCC have been without incident, the relationship with the union representing part-time faculty has been contentious since its origin. The college successfully dealt with two strikes by the adjunct faculty union and stood fast in its last negotiations with the union on significant management and academic issues. A labor dispute that lasted seven years ensued. In the end, because of the resolve of the board and the administration, significant adjustments were made to the part-time faculty's contract. Throughout the negotiations, the press highlighted the issues. Settlement followed only after the college sought and obtained relief in the state's highest court from those contract provisions that threatened the regional accreditation of the college.

Finally, the college has had speakers who have evoked protests from persons outside the campus, thus creating stress for the board and president as they resisted the protesters' demands for a code defining acceptable speech at the college. Through consensus building, the issue was successfully resolved by the board's affirmation of the importance of civility in public discourse while rejecting the call for a speech code.

Each of these issues drew local, state, and national attention; each on its own had the potential for causing major disruptions within the college. But they were dealt with in a manner that reflected well upon the institution and upon a president-board relationship marked by frequent dialogue and discussion.

Important Lessons Learned

To ensure that a crisis does not become a disaster, three things must be done: communicate, communicate, and communicate. Communicate with the board, communicate with the college community, and communicate with the stakeholders. It is imperative that the communication be done effectively; it should be complete and timely. Above all, good communication between the president and the board is necessary in dealing with any crisis. The emphasis, however, is on the effectiveness of the communication; serious harm results from poor or incomplete communication.

Since the president is closer to the institution than are the trustees, it becomes the president's responsibility to take charge of the communication process to ensure that a crisis does not worsen. Should the president fail in that effort, the president-board relationship is no doubt significantly harmed. Nason (1980) supports this position. At the top of his list of thirteen duties of trustees is their responsibility to be informed. It is the president's responsibility to assist trustees in fulfilling that duty, especially during a crisis.

Good communication in a crisis requires a clear and concise description of the event that has precipitated the crisis and the steps that are being taken to deal with it. A cause-and-effect approach is frequently helpful as the president explains to trustees the events or issues leading to the crisis and its impact upon the institution.

Crisis Communications

The predictable, or hurricane-type, crises at Nassau Community College included the two challenges to academic freedom: a demand to cancel performance of a theater department production, and a demand to eliminate a human sexuality course from the college's curriculum. (In both instances, the college had ample warning that a crisis was looming, as small but vocal groups of local residents began organized protests through letters and statements to the press.) Another predictable crisis was foreshadowed by the contentious and drawn-out contract negotiation with the part-time faculty. These events provided an opportunity for precrisis communiqués with the board in which materials associated with the protests and positions taken by the parties were shared. Foremost through these communications, as president I was able to present to the board alternative strategies and positions and to articulate them to the college community and the public at large. Being provided with a recommended response to the unfolding events, the board was able to formulate a position and project a proactive rather than reactive image.

With the crises that come like earthquakes, communication begins as the crisis is unfolding. Because there is little time for precrisis communication, the president must be especially effective in informing the board in these instances. At NCC, the earthquake took the form of a speaker unexpectedly engaging in an anti-Semitic diatribe at an event sponsored by the student government. To minimize the impact of this occurrence, the college had to respond quickly. The president had the responsibility of deciding what action would be taken to correct or minimize the situation. With the knowledge of the board of trustees, the college issued a statement critical of the speaker while encouraging campus groups who invite speakers to be sensitive to the possible hurt that can be engendered by ill-chosen remarks.

Effective Board Communications. In both unanticipated and anticipated crises, the president must begin intense communication with the board as soon as possible. Depending upon the urgency of the issue, communications can be written, oral, or both. All discussions with board members must include the negative ramifications associated with the crisis at hand. Potter (1979) advises the president to avoid communicating only information that supports his or her position. The president must outline every possibility so that there are no surprises for board members. Trustees must therefore be forewarned of even the remotest possibility of disaster. This initial contact with board members may be the most critical phase in all the communication that occurs.

The effectiveness of communication with the board at any point is influenced by the mutual respect and trust that exists between the president and the board (Potter, 1979). If either party lacks this respect and trust, a crisis only serves to intensify an existing, serious problem.

Precrisis Communications. The best time to communicate with the board about a crisis is before it occurs, if at all possible. This requires that the president be constantly on the alert and sensitive to the campus climate. It is, therefore, important to scan the environment before each board meeting and alert board members to any unusual blips on the screen. Advising board members that an issue may be brewing helps prepare them for the actual event, should it occur. For example, the board should be informed if a controversial speaker is coming to campus, if negotiations with the union are not going well, if charges of impropriety are being brought against an administrator or a faculty member, or if enrollment goals will not be reached. The board should then be advised of the steps the president is taking to prevent the issue from escalating. Kerr and Gade (1986) suggest that among the tests of a good president are effective consultation with the board, early discussions of important issues, sharing adequate information, and ensuring that there are never any surprises for trustees. These two threads—good communication and no surprises for trustees—run through most of the work written about president-board relationships.

Communication is two-way: from president to board and from board to president. Potter (1979, p. 50) states: "Nothing is more important than effective communication between the president and the board. A president must keep the board fully informed of everything of any significance involving the college." He continues: "Trustees have a concurrent responsibility to communicate to the president all information the trustees receive regarding the college [that] . . . they have reason to believe is not possessed by the president." A president must carefully weigh input from board members. Although each member contributes to the board, the board is one entity and should speak with one voice. If a president tries to follow the direction of individual members, he or she is doomed to offend those whose advice is not followed. Greenfield (1978) was correct when he warned presidents not to "get along by going along" (p. 35).

If preliminary discussion prior to a board meeting is not possible, a letter or memo sent to board members can alert them to the impending crisis in advance of its becoming public. Such a communiqué can also be an opportunity for board input in crafting a response to the crisis. An added benefit of written communication to the board is that it allows issues to be better clarified and discussions more focused. This procedure gives the president an opportunity to provide all board members with the same information at the same time. It reinforces the good practice of treating all board members equally; nothing is more disconcerting to a trustee than the feeling that his or her peers have more or different information than he or she does regarding a crisis that is unfolding.

The timing of trustee notification is crucial. It is highly detrimental to have a trustee call about a matter that he or she has heard about from members of the media or from a source other than the president or board chair. Protocol and good practice dictate that the chair of the board be notified before the rest of the board is informed. Although some chairs prefer to convey the information to their colleagues on the board themselves, the president may be in a much better position to do so since he or she is closer to the situation and better prepared to answer any questions trustees might have.

After materials have been sent to the trustees, a conference call or individual calls to discuss the matter should take place between and among the president and board members. If the situation permits, there should be no delay in this discussion. Once such information is shared with board members, all recipients should consider it privileged; premature release of this information can have disastrous effects, not the least of which is the dissension that it may engender within the board.

Outlining a Course of Action. A necessary and important element for successfully dealing with a crisis is to have a crisis plan in place and follow it (Koplik, Martin, and Samels, 1996). Koplik suggests developing a crisis audit, which asks whether the institution can detect a crisis at an early stage, whether it is prepared to manage a crisis, and finally, to what extent an institution might benefit from a crisis. A plan minimizes any crisis, but the president must take the lead in drafting such a plan.

During discussions with the trustees, the president must clearly present the plan. The aim is to get firm and unwavering board support. It is therefore incumbent upon the president to make the issue crystal clear and to outline a well-defined plan for the trustees to adopt or support. The plan should be flexible. Because it is often necessary to change directions in a crisis as the result of new or evolving circumstances, the president must be sure to explain the reasons for the change to the board lest the plan be perceived as not being well thought out.

Communicating with the College Community. It is important to notify trustees as early as possible in a crisis, but it is equally important to notify the college community. Once a majority of the board supports a position or plan, the communication phase moves to a new arena, the college community. The president should inform the college community of the issue and the institution's response. The college community should be told of the board's endorsement of the institutional response to the crisis, and of the board's support of the president.

Campbell (1980) reminds us of the ever-present grapevine: "When people are advised of what is happening, why it is happening and what the likely outcome will be, they talk briefly about it, then go on to other things" (p. 111). It may well be that the president needs the help of all or at least some college constituencies in resolving the issue. Of course, the time to enlist that aid is not during a crisis, but before the crisis erupts. Support of campus constituencies is gained and maintained by early and frequent communications.

At NCC, meetings are held regularly with the leaders of various organizations, including the academic senate, unions, and student government. These groups are kept informed of the status of campus issues. When a crisis appears to be brewing, the groups are contacted or consulted. (Doing this gives a "read" on the positions of the various campus groups.) In a time of crisis, a president can never overcommunicate, nor can he or she communicate with too many constituencies.

Informing the Media. Simultaneously with notice to the college community, a press release should be prepared reflecting the board's stand on the crisis at hand. The press release should come from the chair of the board and the president. The chair should be briefed by the college staff about possible questions from the media arising from the press release. The college public relations officer should be fully informed of the events unfolding as well as the actions contemplated by the administration and board to deal with them. At this stage in dealing with a crisis, the president and the public relations officer must be in constant contact with each other.

Who Is the Spokesperson for the Campus? Typically, the president should be the spokesperson for the institution: "Except for unusual situations, the president should speak for the institution. To the extent that someone needs to speak for the board, it is essential for the president and the chairperson to reach an understanding about respective roles" (Zwingle, 1982, pp. 23–24). But there are times when it is in the president's best interest to have the chair speak for the institution: "To the extent that the chairperson as a spokesperson does not invade the functions of administration, the chairperson can serve a good purpose as voice for the board—giving visibility to the board and serving as a buffer for the president" (Zwingle, 1982, p. 24). When the president is under siege by the faculty or the community, the best course of action would be for the chair to speak for the institution.

Communicating with Institutional Sponsors. Once the press is notified, the president should ensure that the sponsors of the institution, including appropriate local and state agencies, are also informed. Usually the task of notifying college sponsors falls to the public relations officer or the governmental liaison officer. Remember, it is important to notify the board members before any of these officials are notified, lest a member of one of these groups becomes the first to contact a board member during a crisis.

Institutional sponsors frequently need to be educated about the scope of their rights and responsibilities. This task falls within the purview of the president, who may enlist the aid of board members close to these officials. For example, some sponsors presume that funding authority includes the right to determine administrative or institutional policy. Educating the sponsor is a process that the president must take as an ongoing responsibility to avoid the need to cram the lesson home during a crisis.

Trustees must be reminded by presidents that they hold the college in trust for the students, not just for those who have appointed them. An illustration involving trustees newly appointed to a state university board underscores the importance of avoiding political intrusion upon higher education. Thomas Bartlett, former chancellor of the State University of New York, observed that trustees who sided with the governor on certain issues rather than acting independently and representing the larger interests of society were not fulfilling their trust. "The board has a responsibility to face the university and insist that it fulfills its obligations to the public," he said. "But it must also face the other direction and buffer the university from politics. The board is the point at which these two spheres intersect. That is a subtle but vital function" (quoted in Arenson, 1996, p. B2).

As in Bartlett's case, the president may find himself or herself having to juggle these two spheres. While doing this, the president must learn to be politic but not political in dealing with trustees and government officials. The president has the unenviable responsibility of keeping both the board and the college out of politics.

Communicating with Other Stakeholders. In situations involving protests from stakeholders, the college must give them an opportunity to share their views. At NCC, this is done by setting aside blocks of time during the public session of board meetings to allow for comment from interested parties. Board members simply listen to the speakers and do not engage them in debate. Although this does not completely satisfy those who are protesting an action by the college or the board, they do feel that the meetings provide them with a forum to voice their concerns. These meetings also allow college personnel to speak. When our curriculum was challenged, faculty and leaders of professional organizations spoke eloquently of the need to preserve academic freedom. Their remarks helped reassure board members that they had made the right decisions.

On the other hand, trustees must be resolute in not engaging in debate with stakeholders during the public session. In the matter of labor negotiations with the part-time union at NCC, the union attempted to use the board meetings as a vehicle to negotiate in public. To its credit, the college board refused to fall for the ploy and remained steadfast in its resolve to take back management prerogatives that had been given up in prior contracts with the union.

The President's Responsibilities. As suggested, the president is the key in resolving a campus crisis. Presidents do not suddenly develop all the necessary skills to deal with boards during a crisis. They must possess those skills before the crisis occurs, and they must have clearly demonstrated them to the board in day-to-day operations of the college.

The same holds true for trustees. It is too late to educate trustees about their roles and responsibilities during a crisis. Educating trustees is an ongoing responsibility of the president, part of the "care and feeding" of trustees. If trustees have been regularly informed, if they have been consulted on important matters, if they have been heard during board sessions, then a crisis does not cause a significant departure from business as usual. If, however, it takes a crisis to generate genuine dialogue with board members, then the current crisis is a minor matter; the presidential relationship with the board is a far greater campus problem.

The political nature of the board must not be overlooked. In spite of the best efforts to keep politics out of the board room, it exists there nonetheless. In a crisis, the president must help assure that board members are not captured by special groups such as faculty unions, student organizations, or community leaders.

Trustees' Responsibilities. Trustees also have clear responsibilities in times of campus difficulty. Trustees should work together to develop a clear position and take definitive action regarding the crisis. Finally, there is the need for trustees to speak with one voice through the chair or the president. Once the president and the board have built a consensus position, it must be articulated as the position of the board. The board speaks with only one voice.

If they publicly share their opposition to the board's position, individual board members make it more difficult, or perhaps impossible, to resolve a campus problem. It is not difficult for them to gain an audience. The media is all too willing to write a story of controversy rather than consensus. Whereas board members have a first amendment right to air their personal views, their responsibilities as trustees of the institution should not be forgotten. This is especially true when comments are made for personal gain. If ever there is a time when the diplomacy of the president is tested, it is when she or he must disagree with a trustee in public or in the media.

Never Take a Crisis for Granted. If not dealt with quickly and effectively, some crises can have a lasting effect upon the campus community. While they tax the mental and physical resources of the president and board, when handled effectively most crises become memories in a few months. Common sense dictates that the fewer crises a board must deal with, the happier it is. Too many crises that require involving the board may be a signal that the president is not capable of handling the everyday administrative tasks of the institution. In a crisis of the president's own making, the board quickly recognizes that it may be symptomatic of a lack of managerial or leadership skills. Even when the crisis is solved, an enlightened board may come to see the president as the genesis of the problem.

The story is told of the sailor who is given a medal by the captain for lashing down a cannon, at great personal risk, as it threatens to sink the ship by rolling back and forth on deck during a storm. No sooner has the medal been awarded than the captain orders the same sailor thrown in the brig because it was his responsibility to secure the cannon before the storm. Much can be learned from the story. In times of crisis, the president must not be caught lashing down the cannon. Rather, the effective president has already done the lashing and is prepared to weather the storm. Boards quickly recognize when a president is solving crises of his or her own making.

Crises Can Bring out the Best in an Institution

A sense of shared responsibility can rally the board around a course of action. Crisis situations can bring out the best in trustees if the situation is handled properly by the president and the board. If there are tensions between the board and various groups on campus, then it is the president who must build bridges. This is especially true with faculty: "It is the president—as leader, manager, and above all teacher—who must establish common ground between the concerns of trustees and of faculty" (Taylor, 1995, p. 9). A crisis in which campus constituencies join with the board strengthens board-campus relationships. In these situations, the president and the board emerge as true leaders who demonstrate a caring vision for the entire campus community.

Every crisis offers the president and the board an opportunity to learn important leadership lessons. A thorough review of the sequence of events, the institutional responses, and campus and community reactions must be undertaken as soon as the dust clears. Communication links must be analyzed to determine their effectiveness. This postmortem review greatly strengthens the president-board relationship.

Constantly working to improve the relationship does much to prepare any president or board for the eventuality of a crisis. Ingram (1996, p. 50) is correct when he contends that "the vast majority of chief executives and governing boards are coping successfully with very difficult issues and that their relationships are fundamentally, even incredibly, sound." While that is true in many cases, it does not happen without effective communication between the parties.

Finally, one of the president's responsibilities is to make the board look good, especially in a crisis situation. Nason (1974) provides a capstone comment: "Board effectiveness depends on the president and on the relations between the president and the board. The wise president keeps his board fully informed—about mistakes as well as successes and about whatever problems require immediate or long-range solution. Complete candor, mutual respect, and a willingness to support the president are ingredients in effective governance" (Nason, 1974, p. 2). If this advice is followed, the president surely looks good as well.

References

Arenson, K. W. "What Went Wrong at SUNY?" *New York Times,* July 29, 1996, p. B2.

Campbell, D. *If I'm in Charge Here Why Is Everybody Laughing?* Greensboro, N.C.: Center for Creative Leadership, 1980.

Greenfield, R. K. "The President as Politician." *Community and Junior College Journal,* 1978, 48 (7), 34–36.

Ingram, R. T. "New Tensions in the Academic Boardroom." *Educational Record,* 1996, 77 (2, 3), 49–55.

Kerr, C., and Gade, M. L. *The Many Lives of Academic Presidents: Time, Place, and Character.* Washington, D.C.: Association of Governing Boards of Universities and Colleges, 1986.

Koplik, S. Z., Martin, J., and Samels, J. E. "In a Crisis, Count to 10." *Trusteeship,* 1996, 4 (1), 22–26.

Nason, J. W. *The Future of Trusteeship: The Role and Responsibilities of College and University Boards.* Washington, D.C.: Association of Governing Boards of Universities and Colleges, 1974.

Potter, G. E. *Trusteeship: Handbook for Community College and Technical Institute Trustees.* Washington, D.C.: Association of Community College Trustees, 1979.

Taylor, B. E. (ed.). "A Calling to Account." *Priorities,* Summer 1995, no. 4, 1–15.

Zwingle, J. L. *Effective Trusteeship.* Washington, D.C.: Association of Governing Boards of Universities and Colleges, 1982.

SEAN A. FANELLI is president of Nassau Community College in Garden City, New York.

Increasingly, when a college faces a crisis it must also face the glare of public scrutiny. Poor leadership during a crisis can be devastating and can cause major changes in day-to-day operations. For the president and the governing board team to function effectively during a time of crisis, the key is planning and management.

When a Crisis Occurs:
A Trustee's Perspective

Phyllis Gutierrez Kenney

A crisis is defined as "a decisive or crucial moment." During the last decade, some new words have crept into the lexicon of academe, although we might wish they had not. Along with *crisis,* the words *disaster* and *catastrophe* no longer pertain solely to incidents in our natural environment. Once associated with hurricanes, fires, and floods, they may even characterize the everyday life of our community colleges.

Crisis management, crisis communication, and crisis planning should be critical components in an institution's strategic planning. Any college crisis can have an adverse impact on the college family and the community. A crisis can be anything from loss of funding to botched news coverage or dismissal of an administrator. Each can have the effect of setting off a chain of events that involve staff time and money. How would your campus react if, for example, it was revealed that your college president was under FBI investigation? What would happen if your president then became incommunicado and ultimately had to be replaced on short notice? Would your board have a policy in place to deal with presidential misconduct? Would you know who could step in as interim president on a moment's notice? How would your campus continue to function? Would your donors continue to give? Would the faculty and staff stick with the institution?

This example is not far fetched. Similar events happened in my state (Washington), and it was a quick-thinking, experienced, and prepared board of trustees that kept the campus operating smoothly, events on schedule, and short- and long-term plans in effect.

Ideally, trustees work with the administration, the faculty, and the students to produce an institution of such educational excitement, with such a sense of momentum, that a crisis is unlikely to arise. That is the ideal world. It is not realistic, because we all know that crises, both internal and external, occur occasionally, sometimes more often than desired. How do we establish a response team, if you will, to curb the situation immediately and minimize the damage? Someone once said that governing a community or technical college is like riding a bicycle: in order to maintain your equilibrium, you have to keep moving forward. In a crisis, you must be ready to move forward. Boards and institutions that are well prepared to move forward perform best in a crisis.

Crisis Management Plan

Experienced trustees will tell you that a crisis is like any natural disaster, often unavoidable but something you can plan for and learn from. There are a broad range of situations in which institutions require a mechanism that identifies and responds to crisis issues. For each situation, there should be some type of crisis management model. Certain disastrous situations can be avoided through effective planning. For example, planning can ease transitions surrounding a change of president or chancellor; it can prevent or shorten a faculty strike. Crisis management plans can be instrumental in easing some of the destructive effects of even the most unforeseeable crisis.

A college kite-flying contest turned into a disaster at one community college when a kite string wrapped around the ankle of a contestant. The wind lifted him into the air and flung him to the ground, killing him. The action plan in place allowed the institution to be sympathetic in the face of the tragedy, but to minimize the long-term negative effect of the tragedy on the college's reputation.

Through the leadership of the president and trustees, institutions should ensure that a crisis management plan is in place—first to deter avoidable emergencies, and second to plan for the unavoidable ones. A crisis management plan provides the institution with the ability to continue its day-to-day operations while the crisis is being managed.

Certain characteristics make up an effective plan:

The plan must be doable. If a plan cannot be effectively implemented and carried out, it isn't worth the paper it is written on.
The plan must be understandable. Keep it simple.
The plan must be reviewed with all personnel who are affected.
The plan must include a list of key players, with their telephone, pager, and cellular telephone numbers. It quite often happens that the simple, logistical part of an operation is omitted from the plan.
The plan must be reviewed regularly to ensure that it is working effectively.
The plan must be comprehensive but flexible enough to accommodate every possibility that may arise. A good crisis plan should only be used as the framework by which the president and the board consider issues and make informed decisions.

Crisis management should not require that all personnel stop work to address each crisis. Instead, crises should be handled with minimal interference in the day-to-day routine. In the case of the investigated president, the crisis plan kept the campus running smoothly, without much awareness that the president was out of touch with the college.

Components of a Crisis Management Plan

Some elements are imperative to a good crisis management plan. Trustees and the president need to review the key elements that play an important part in the plan's success.

Governance. Unless there is clear understanding about the role of trustees as policy makers and the administration as the agent for carrying out those policies, when a crisis develops, the board-president relationship may already be in jeopardy. Experience has told us that when a campus is in a crisis situation, there is a better chance of resolving the situation promptly if lines of authority and responsibility between the president and the board are already clearly established and accepted. Neither the board nor the president needs the added burden of developing working relationships while trying to put out fires. Having had eight children, I look at preparedness like family fire drills: be sure everyone knows what to do in case the house catches fire.

Trustees are continually reminded that they are not to meddle in administration. Yet they often do not make the comparable call when the administration moves into the policy arena. For example, trustees may find out after the fact that their college has purchased property, denying them their responsibility of setting policy around such purchases. If appropriate roles are not respected, an internal crisis can have a fallout effect on operations. It is important, therefore, that the president and trustees work together to ensure that they have a common understanding of their respective roles in the effective, and shared, governance of their institution.

Communication. In any crisis situation, communication is the key. A first response to any crisis situation might be concern about what others are saying about the college. But before we worry about the media, we need to worry about how we are communicating with each other. Communication is an important part of crisis management. It allows for an orderly response to crisis situations. Remember that communication is not only speaking but listening as well.

Trustee-President Communications. Each institution has its own communication model, based on experience and personalities among other factors. At some institutions, the president may relay crisis information first to the board chair and then to other members of the board. At other community colleges, the chair may be responsible for informing the other board members about the crisis. My experience as a trustee suggests that information should be relayed to all the board members by the president. Regardless of who relays the information, it is important that all trustees be informed of the crisis and administrative actions as they occur. Keeping the trustees informed builds support and strength for the ultimate resolution of the problem.

The worst possible scenario is when the president has not been informed of the status of the crisis. If an internal or external crisis arises or even threatens to arise, the chief defender of the college is the president or chancellor, the person who must move with speed and initiative, with courage, firmness, and fairness. The president or chancellor should turn to his or her board of trustees as an insulating force to help preserve and protect the integrity of the institution. Trustees should neither expect nor be expected by the president to stand on the sidelines and watch the show. Trustees should support the president as he or she carries out board policy. They need to listen to the facts and issues and advise the administration of their best judgment as the crisis moves on to resolution.

The board as a whole should communicate to the president the issues of concern regarding the course of action proposed or being taken. In some cases, trustees may not agree among themselves about how a situation is being handled. Board members have an obligation to listen to all sides and have an honest discussion of all of the issues. Internal disagreements among trustees must be dealt with before the "real" crisis gets out of control.

The president and board should speak from the same script to the media, the community college family, and the community. In order to do this, the president and the board must communicate with each other clearly and in a timely manner about the issues relating to the crisis and the agreed-upon plan of action.

Who Speaks? The most effective crisis plan calls for one trustee to be designated as the spokesperson. Generally the spokesperson is the board chair, but if the chair doesn't feel that he or she is in the best position to do so or is not comfortable with the subject, another trustee may be chosen. The spokesperson should be well informed, and communication between the president and the spokesperson should be ongoing.

All trustees must adhere to the agreement that there is only one spokesperson. Unfortunately, this does not always occur, and sometimes a trustee other than the spokesperson chooses to give opinions or comments to the media or the community. The spokesperson must use discipline in response to the media, college members, and the community. The spokesperson should not defend or dispute what the other trustee has said but should bring attention back to the message agreed upon by the board and the president. The next step is to call the trustee in for a cup of coffee and a frank discussion about the overstepping of boundaries. Situations like these must be avoided, for they can cause the board and the president to lose credibility within the college and the community.

As trustees, we have more influence than we think. We can play a pivotal role in a crisis. Unfortunately, we can also tip the balance in a significant way that may not be to the benefit of the institution if we are careless or not aware of our responsibilities. Play by the rules.

Community College Family. A good management plan must include consultation and involvement with the members of the community college family.

There should be a plan on how the president, working with representative leadership of the campus constituencies or trustees, communicates to the community college members about the crisis issues and about what is being done to resolve them. Whatever form of communication is used, be sure that it is clear, simple, and honest. In the case of a faculty strike, a daily news bulletin might be in order. The president or trustees might have an open forum for college employees. An example can illustrate the importance of formal communication with the college faculty and staff. During a strike at one community college, a staff person in athletics told the local newspaper that the college's sports events would continue as planned—the exact opposite of what the college president and trustees had determined. They had simply failed to tell athletics—or anyone else on campus—how business would proceed during the strike.

Another concern during trying times is whether trustees should meet with groups or individuals involved in the crisis. To just say no is shortsighted; the door should never be closed. Trustees have a responsibility to listen, evaluate, and take seriously what is being said. However, this should be done within the guidelines and procedures of the policies that the board has set forth for dealing with disputes and crises. An individual trustee should not imply that he or she personally is going to do something about the situation. This kind of action counteracts the problem-solving approach essential to working out a solution. It not only erodes the internal working relationships of the board but also undermines the role and authority of the president.

Communicating with the Community and the Media. A strong community communications plan is essential. Chances are that the crisis requires the college to respond to the public in a variety of ways. Statements to the community and the media are important and must be clear and precise, staying as close as possible to the message. Be sure the information being released is timely. Releases should be authorized by the president, and board members should be kept informed of all press releases and public statements. When the board spokesperson makes the release or statement, the full board must be in concurrence.

Training—or even rehearsals—provide the spokesperson with an opportunity to practice responding to unanticipated questions. For example, rehearsing would have been helpful when a president of one community college gave an interview during a faculty strike. As the reporter put away his notebook, he asked what would happen if the strike were not resolved in a timely fashion. The president shrugged and in an off-hand manner said that if the strike were not resolved, the college would cancel the quarter. That off-the-cuff statement became the headline and the lead paragraph the next morning. Instead of being able to work toward resolving the strike, the president spent the day doing damage control with the campus, the board, and the media. Remember that reporters are not required to read you your Miranda rights. And, unfortunately, a controversy makes a better news story than does a resolution.

What Happens When the President Is the Center of the Crisis? Nothing is more disruptive to the college and the community than when the president or chancellor is the focal point of the crisis. At one community college, the president of nearly twenty years retired and his successor changed everything from parking rules to administrative structure, causing turmoil on campus. Still, the new president had the board's support and was even granted a contract renewal. But internal conflict over the changes persisted, until a group of college retirees and other "friends" of the institution pressured the governor to appoint a task force to study the turmoil. At the same time, two new trustees who had been appointed to fill board vacancies changed the board from one of unified support to one of divided loyalties. The two new members worked independently of the other board members, investigated the president on their own, and eventually convinced a third trustee to abandon support for the president. Since this was a five-member board, this alliance changed the course of action that the board eventually took.

The changes in the college leadership and in board composition left the institution unprepared for the first crisis in the college's history. The nature of the crisis—the conflicts between the president and the campus, and between the president and the board—further muddled the ability of either the president or the board to resolve the situation. After nearly a year, the board bought out the renewed contract and replaced the president in conflict with a more conciliatory interim president.

These college trustees started out on the right track with a plan of action. They worked together and spoke with one voice, as a board must, when faced with a crisis. But the addition of the new trustees broke the board's solidarity. The trustees momentarily forgot that as individuals they have no standing—that their influence and authority derive from the group. Yet, in the end, they were able to regroup, and ultimately it was their unity that resolved the situation.

Using Data for Decision Making

Boards should strive to identify the issues related to the crisis and assess the impact that these issues have on the college and the community. An integral part of this process is information gathering. Information should be gathered from all possible sources. Your plan must be very specific on how you gather the facts. If you are going to hear from different groups, do it as a board or a committee of the board. The community college in the above example gathered their information with the help of a task force. The state-appointed task force met with more than sixty people and collected a six-foot-high stack of documents from three days of interviews. It was the work of the task force, and not of individual trustees, that led to resolution of the crisis. It is dangerous for individual trustees to act as the sounding board for differing viewpoints. To repeat: an individual trustee implying that he or she personally is going to correct a situation only adds confusion and frustration to an already stressful situation.

Often overlooked as valuable resources are the trustees and administrators of other community colleges that are similar in size and programs to the college where a crisis has occurred. Learn from those who have experienced a similar situation. Measure the experience and methods used by others against your own situation. In Washington, we have established a team approach program to provide assistance to each other when requested. There is a wealth of experience and expertise among our college trustees. We need to use it—for our own benefit!

Conclusion

The keys to crisis management are planning, preparation, and a strong working relationship between the president and the board. Cooperation between the president and the board is essential when the pressure is on. The foundation for how a board and president work together during a time of crisis is established long before the crisis occurs. They must work continuously to build trust and confidence in each other and in their ability to be good stewards of the institution they serve.

One way to develop that relationship may be to set aside one work session each year to review and amend the crisis plan. Trustees and presidents may wish to take time during that session to practice their interview skills or to role play a crisis situation. A review of the college's history, noting how crises were handled or averted, can also provide valuable insight and highlight ways to improve the plan. In addition, it might be useful to discuss how trustees at other colleges handled their crises, or invite one or two trustees from other community colleges to the session to share their experiences and what they learned. Whether the board changes member by member each year or changes its entire membership at once, it is important that the crisis plan be learned and reviewed regularly. Thorough preparation by the president and the board to respond to a crisis can minimize the adversity and its consequences.

PHYLLIS GUTIERREZ KENNEY is a trustee with the Seattle Community College District. She is the past president of the Washington State Trustees Association in Seattle.

*The upcoming millennium provides presidents and trustees with
the opportunity to consider the current state of community college
governance and its implication for refocusing presidents' and trustees'
contributions to their community colleges.*

At the Millennium

Fred Gaskin

Those of us associated with community colleges tend to look at decade
changes as opportunities to pause and consider how we might better serve our
students. We discuss not only what we should be doing but also how we are
doing it. Throughout my career, which began in the early 1970s, I have participated in task forces labeled "Renewal for the Eighties," "Strategies for the
Nineties," and, recently, "Vision 2000." While the topics have been different,
a common theme has been that a change in the decade provides significant
opportunity for contemplating possible changes in how community college
leaders fulfill their roles.

The upcoming millennium has stirred those of us in community college
leadership positions to reflect on the changes that need to occur to ensure that
our institutions continue to provide quality education and service for our students. This chapter examines the evolution of community college governance
over the last few decades. Suggestions follow on how presidents and trustees
might adjust our focus in response to these changes in governance and to the
needs of the students we are privileged to serve.

Whereas there is general agreement that the primary role of the president
and trustees is governance, there is much debate about what governance
means. Determining where to draw the line between governance and operations is a frequent discussion at many community colleges. There is also much
debate about the role of others besides the president and trustees in the governance of our colleges. What is clear, though, is that presidents' and trustees'
roles in college governance are changing. It is also clear that external forces—
primarily state legislatures—and internal constituency groups—primarily the
faculty—are playing a much more significant role in college governance. The
expanded role of these two groups in particular diminishes the traditional role
for presidents and trustees.

Those of us who serve as either community college presidents or members of governing boards have a responsibility to bring value-added to the organization that we serve. Only then can we justify our place in the organization and the trust placed in us by those who afford us the opportunity to hold our positions. We should constantly ask ourselves, "How is this college better able to meet the needs of its constituency because of my contribution? What am I doing to position the college both for the present and for the years to come?" For better or for worse, community colleges are forever different because of the impact that presidents and boards have on them.

Over the past decade, the role of governance within community colleges has dramatically changed. How did this change in governance evolve? In many instances, the evolution has been the result of state legislation mandating changes in governance structures or shifting certain responsibilities that previously were under the purview of the local college board to the state.

For California, changes in governance were accelerated with the passage of Proposition 13 in 1979. Prop 13 moved the funding responsibilities for community colleges from a strong local base to a strong state base. Of course, once the state had more funding responsibility, it began to exercise more control over college operations. The result was a reduction in the decision-making authority of local college boards that continues today.

Another prime example of changes in governance, also in California, is the impact that AB 1725 had on the structure of governance within the community colleges of California. This landmark 1988 legislation stipulated that the governance of the colleges be shared with internal constituency groups. The foremost internal group is the faculty. AB 1725 listed eleven areas of governance in which the president and local board either rely primarily upon, or consult collegially with, the faculty. Examples include curriculum development, including degree and certificate requirements; grading policies; institutional planning and budget development; and selection, evaluation, and retention of faculty. The legislation also mandated shared governance agreements with other employee groups as well as with students. In other states, legislatures have mandated general education requirements, maximum credits for degrees, the joining together of technical colleges and community colleges, and faculty teaching loads, among other intrusions into areas previously within the traditional responsibility of local college boards.

In addition, state funding is tending to move toward more categorical or program-specific allocations than has traditionally been the case. The effect of such funding is that colleges are becoming more similar to each other, rather than being designed to meet the unique needs of their constituency. At many community college districts, for example, there are far more categorical or "earmarked" dollars than there are discretionary funds in the budget.

These examples of legislation demonstrate how the function of presidents and boards has changed dramatically. The effect is that although community colleges are moving to a more collegial or traditional college and university system of governance for internal operations, greater control is being exercised from the state level. The paradox begs the following questions: What is the role of the president and board? How do we provide the value-added to justify our positions?

In the next millennium, no single factor will be more important to the successful functioning of a community college than a mutually supportive relationship between a board of trustees and its president. To be mutually supportive, presidents and boards must clearly understand their own roles and each other's. This is not to suggest, though, that a clear delineation between the roles is always present. To be sure, there is more blending of these roles than there is a clear differentiation, a situation that often causes a significant degree of ambiguity. Tolerating or accepting ambiguity itself requires a level of understanding and trust achieved only through open and forthright dialogue, not just between the president and board but also throughout the entire college community.

Working as a team, trustees and presidents should focus on three areas of activity: guarding access, pursuing alternative funding sources, and engaging in political and civic activities. In addition, trustees and presidents must capitalize on their own unique talents and experiences to enhance college operations. This focus allows presidents and trustees to continue to be of value to their organizations as governing systems evolve.

Guarding Access

First, presidents and trustees must be the primary guardians of the egalitarian philosophy of the community college. As affirmative action programs come under attack from many quarters, we must remember that community colleges hold a unique place in higher education. In remarks delivered at the American Council on Education's annual meeting in February 1996, Robert Atwell said, "Higher education should be about values—the values of informed citizenship, the values expressed in a sense of responsibility toward those whose potential has not been realized for reasons not of their own doing." It is this "sense of responsibility toward those whose potential has not been realized" that is the principal mission of American community colleges. For the vast majority of our students, there simply is not a good answer to the question, "If not the community college, then what?" For them, there simply is no possible higher education alternative.

The responsibility of protecting access for those who most need community colleges rests with the presidents and trustees. We must be the ones to fight assiduously to ensure that the mission of the community colleges remains intact. We must be the ones to protect the unique nature of the community colleges not only when access is challenged but when necessary support services and systems are threatened. Yet it is not enough to simply let everyone into the institution. The challenge is to let them in and provide them with the necessary tools to complete their education successfully. In Florida, for example, legislation denies funding for repeating a remedial class because of a failing grade. If a student fails a remedial class, the entire cost of repeating the class must be paid by the student. For regular credit courses, there is no penalty of this type for failing. When the question is asked, "How many times do I have to pay to teach Johnny to read?" the answer for community colleges has to be "one more time." Presidents and trustees must be the ones who speak for the millions of individuals who have the potential to benefit from attending community colleges.

Pursuing Alternative Funding Sources

The importance of alternative fund development is going to become critical as we move into the next century. Throughout all of higher education, there will likely continue to be a reduction in traditional sources of funding. Public funding, as a percentage of total budget, has been going down for years; yet, the needs of our students are greater and the costs for providing for them continues to rise. Although community college presidents and boards know this, too few see fundraising as part of their responsibility. If we are to meet the students' needs, we must begin to see alternative fund development as a key responsibility. In this regard, we must emulate the behavior of presidents and trustees from traditional colleges and universities. At a few community colleges, private fundraising has been incorporated into the duties of presidents and trustees with some measure of success. It is not enough for presidents and trustees to simply manage what funds flow to the institution. We have to be proactive in the pursuit of funds in order to meet the needs of our students. This effort not only requires a commitment of time and effort on the part of presidents and trustees, it requires a commitment of institutional resources to achieve this task. Fundraising is expensive. Traditional colleges and universities understand this. Frequently, those associated with community colleges have difficulty understanding the necessary investment.

Engaging in Political and Civic Activities

Community college trustees are frequently active in local politics. Many were elected to their positions. Others were appointed to their positions by elected officials. Consequently the vast majority of community college trustees have some political experience. Some trustees are also on boards other than at colleges, thus providing additional connections with civic organizations. An important role that trustees can play, then, is as informal lobbyists for political and civic causes that have an impact on the college. Since the trustees are known and respected by other political and civic leaders, they can be effective in their lobbying endeavors. The challenge in dealing with political issues is to not let partisan politics interfere with the process of supporting college initiatives. Elected trustees are generally on a nonpartisan ballot. In most instances, however, they are elected on a ballot that includes partisan offices. This is becoming even truer as states move to consolidate elections in an effort to control costs. Appointed trustees, on the other hand, generally share the same party affiliation as those who appoint them. In either case, the important matter is to keep the college and its initiatives outside of partisan politics to the fullest possible extent.

In exchange for state resources, legislatures and governors are imposing changes on community colleges. A good example of this control is Illinois. In both fiscal years 1994 and 1995, public colleges in Illinois received the budget increase they requested. Accompanying these increases, however, was legislation that changed the system of governance for a number of the colleges and universities. As matters of this type are considered by legislators and other politicians, it is important for trustees to have a prominent place in these discussions—and this place goes much further than simply writing letters of support or opposition for the issue. Trustees need to be at the table when the issue is being discussed. Trustees and presidents should even formulate ideas that can be developed into legislative proposals to enhance our colleges' ability to serve students.

Presidential and trustee involvement in local civic activities is equal in importance to their political involvement. A strong relationship with high school districts, for example, is an essential element of a successful community college. This relationship should begin between the governing boards and presidents. When the relationship is strong, it sends a loud signal to members of the college community that it is essential to the college's success. A positive, mutually supportive relationship is also important between the city in which the college is located and the community college. In one instance, the city manager and two council members meet monthly with the college president and two trustees for an informal breakfast meeting where they exchange current information about both college and city matters. Moreover, they discuss ways in which the city and college can work together on a wide range of issues, from economic development to special programming for senior citizens.

Trustees should be active along with the president in the local chamber of commerce and local service clubs. These organizations have much to offer the college and also much to gain from the college. It can be an ideal partnership if pursued properly. The key, however, is the notion of partnership. Presidents and trustees need to understand that along with other community leaders, we contribute not only college resources but also our own personal time and energy. This personal commitment yields significant returns to both the college and the community.

Capitalizing on Special Talents

Trustees frequently have a professional life in addition to being on the college board. Likewise, presidents often have unique professional skills. Presidents and board members need to inventory their talents and utilize them to strengthen our colleges. As suggested above, many trustees have connections in the community that can serve to strengthen relations between the college and the community. Some trustees, through their professional knowledge, can bring expertise to the board and to the college. This is not to suggest, for example, that an attorney on a board should provide legal advice. He or she can, however, assist the college in understanding legal issues and the consequences of certain actions. Likewise, a trustee with solid planning experience can be a major asset in shaping the planning process for the college. A strong background in finance or marketing and public relations experience can be very useful to the college too. The challenge to trustees with this involvement is to keep the activities at the policy level and not participate in management of the college. By utilizing trustees' special talents without crossing over from policy to administration, presidents and trustees can maximize their contributions and minimize ambiguity of roles.

Conclusion

As we approach the twenty-first century, community colleges are going to become even more important to American society. At the national level, more attention has been given to the two-year collegiate experience than ever before. The number of students who need two-year colleges is expanding at a rapid rate. For example, by the year 2005, it is projected that California community colleges will need to serve half a million more students than they serve today. The ultimate responsibility for meeting this expanded need rests with the local presidents and boards of trustees. While it is clear that the governance of our community colleges will be shared principally with faculty members and the state legislatures, this sharing should not lessen the value that presidents and trustees bring to their colleges.

The presidents and trustees need to direct their attention to pursuing open access, seeking alternative revenue sources, and maintaining an active role in the political and civic arena. Further, presidents and trustees need to capitalize on their unique talents and experience to advance the ability of their college to meet the needs of the students whom they serve. The effect of these activities will make a substantial positive impact on the ability of our community colleges to meet the needs of their students into the next millennium.

FRED GASKIN is president/superintendent of the Cerritos Community College District in Norwalk, California. He has been a community college chief executive officer since 1982.

An annotated bibliography provides abstracts of documents from the ERIC system focusing on leadership issues in the community college, and the relationship between presidents and boards.

Sources and Information: Community College Leadership

Lucy Lee

Community college presidents and trustees are at the forefront of higher education's efforts to fulfill an increasingly broad and complex mission. They face unparalleled challenges as leaders of "democracy's colleges."

It may be helpful to view those particular challenges within the broader context of research on organizational leadership in general. The study of leadership has followed a trajectory that can be loosely divided into three time periods. Until World War II, effective leadership was seen, in relatively simplistic terms, as emerging from personality traits that separated the leaders from the followers. The emphasis on trait theory was gradually replaced by a focus on distinctive leadership behaviors. Researchers thought that they could identify the "best" leaders by their style, for example, task-oriented versus relationship-oriented. Behaviorism was dominant in the study of leadership until the early 1960s. Increasingly, researchers in the last thirty years have viewed leadership from the contingency perspective. Contingency theorists assert that the most effective leadership is not defined by any single quality or behavior; rather, truly excellent leaders are willing to adapt their approach based on a given situation or set of circumstances (Wren, 1995). It is worth noting that this shift in the study of leadership occurred at roughly the same time as the rapid growth and diversification of our higher education system since 1960. It seems clear that this model is a better fit for the fluid, dynamic world of higher education in general—and community colleges in particular.

Arguing that most leadership theory mistakenly presupposes that organizations are rationally structured entities, Bensimon (1994) expands on the notion of a situational model for leadership. The structure of a college or university, despite tidy organizational charts, is defined by change and shifting goals, not to mention the constant flow of new students. Administrative leadership must be collaborative and inclusive in order to respond to this constant state of flux. The social change model of leadership development (Higher Education Research Institute, 1996) offers a strategy for achieving the often elusive goal of genuinely collaborative leadership in our colleges and universities. Central to this task is the belief that leadership is a process rather than a position, and that the best leadership decisions are influenced by a foundation of values shared among diverse individuals.

The following publications reflect ERIC literature on leadership in the community colleges. As was pointed out earlier in this volume, presidents and their boards are not always viewed as members of the same leadership team. These citations offer more information regarding practical guidelines for training leaders, the critical responsibility of building relationships with the community, and the role of faculty in leading community colleges. The final section of this chapter provides the latest ERIC literature in which community college leaders look ahead to the challenges and changes of the next century.

ERIC Documents (those referenced with "ED" numbers) can be read on microfiche at approximately nine hundred libraries worldwide. In addition, most may be ordered on microfiche or in hard copy from the ERIC Document Reproduction Service (EDRS) at 800/443-ERIC. All citations preceded by an asterisk (*) refer to journal articles, which are not available from EDRS. Journal articles may be acquired through regular library channels or purchased from article clearinghouses such as CARL Uncover at 800/787-7979 or the UMI Articles Clearinghouse at 800/248-0360. For a list of libraries in your area that house ERIC microfiche documents, an EDRS order form, or more information about our products and services, please contact the ERIC Clearinghouse for Community Colleges at 800/832-8256, or via the Internet at ericcc@ucla.edu.

Practical Guidelines for Effective Leadership

Community College League of California. *Trustee Handbook*. Sacramento: Community College League of California, 1996. (ED 396 792)

Intended as a resource for trustees at California community colleges and those providing training to trustees, this handbook reviews the roles and responsibilities associated with trusteeship. General information on California's community colleges and other systems of higher education sets the scene for a broader discussion of the board as a governing entity, and the responsibilities of individual trustees. A discussion of effective trusteeship includes trustee ethics, board self-evaluation procedures, and effective processes for making decisions. One chapter focuses on board and chief executive officer relations, including conducting CEO searches, evaluation methods, and providing support to CEOs; another chapter reviews regulations and implementation issues related to shared governance. The board's function in community and public relations, fundraising, and political advocacy is discussed. Both the legal and fiscal responsibilities of the community college board are examined, as well as issues of devising standards for minimum qualifications and tenure for board members.

Dowdy, H. B. *A Manual for Trustees: Role, Responsibilities, Relationships.* Cary: North Carolina Association of Community College Trustees, 1996. 62 pp. (ED 388 374)

This manual provides information on trustees' roles, responsibilities, and relationships with other agencies in the state. Following a historical overview of the North Carolina community college system and a review of fourteen significant studies of the system, the key elements of trustees' responsibilities are described. Included are establishing the mission and goals of the institution; appointing, evaluating, and terminating the president; ensuring that the institution is well managed; approving budgets; raising money for programs and facilities; establishing educational programs; approving long-range plans; assisting with public relations efforts; and serving as both a buffer from external pressures and a court of appeal for system policy. A discussion follows, focusing on the trustees' working relationships with the board chair, college presidents, administrative staff, faculty, students, state board members, community college system president and state-level administration, and the state attorney general's office.

Doser, B. "Effective Board/President Relations." Paper presented at an in-service meeting of the Michigan Community College Association, Feb. 2–3, 1990. 7 pp. (ED 346 889)

College presidents have often been described as the "visionaries" responsible for shaping institutional objectives and matching talents with resources to realize strategic goals. College governing boards are often seen as critical to providing the continuity and stability necessary to guarantee the integrity of the college. A board retreat with the president and all trustees present is suggested as an ideal way to introduce new trustees or a new president, and to impart the values and vision of the institution. Boards and presidents jointly develop a clear common vision, as well as outline the priorities for the institution. Then boards should stand back, offering constructive challenges and support, as the president expands and builds upon the collective vision for the college.

Lamb, B., and others. "Delivering the 'Write' Message: The Memo and Transformational Leadership." In *The Olympics of Leadership: Overcoming Obstacles, Balancing Skills, Taking Risks.* Proceedings of the fifth annual International Conference of the National Community College Chair Academy, Phoenix, Ariz., Feb. 14–17, 1996. 8 pp. (ED 394 558)

Leaders must avoid misunderstandings in written communication with key partners in the community college enterprise. No matter what the nature of the written correspondence, college leaders must remember that when a "sender" forms a message and channels this information to a "receiver," communication breakdowns can occur either through mistakenly encoding and decoding information or through language barriers and cultural differences. Further, leaders must be conscious that written communication lacks the cues used in oral communication to refine and interpret the meaning of the message. When the written word is "decoded" in a way that is at odds with the sender's intent, the resulting misunderstanding can provoke emotional responses or unnecessary conflict, thereby wasting precious time. Leaders should ask themselves if the purpose of a written memorandum might be better served though a telephone call or visit. They should also be careful of the tone they adopt in the "voice" behind the memo, always taking into consideration the point of view of the memo's intended audience.

Building Relationships

Rosenthal, L. B., and Elsner, P. "Reinventing Governance: Maricopa Conducts Strategic Conversations." Paper presented at the seventy-sixth annual convention of the American Association of Community Colleges, Atlanta, Ga., Apr. 13–16, 1996. 17 pp. (ED 395 646)

The governing board of Arizona's Maricopa County Community College District (MCCCD) has developed a strategic conversations format to ensure interaction with the college community and continuous quality improvement in the governance process. The use of strategic conversations facilitates communication with the off-campus community, to help constituents understand issues facing the district; the process also informs and guides governing board decision making. Strategic conversations are publicized as informal, open meetings of college personnel, internal and external constituents, and members of the community. Meeting topics are decided in advance by the governing board, usually after conducting a survey on topics of concern to participants. After a brief presentation of the issue to be discussed at the beginning of the strategic conversation, facilitators assist in guiding the exchange of ideas, usually in small break-out groups. The use of strategic conversations has resulted in new institutional diversity policies; a new vision statement; a revised statement of mission, values, and goals; and a climate of open communication and inclusiveness at the MCCCD. Appendices list positive results from the effort, as well as the barriers to implementing the strategic conversations format.

Miller, H. M. "Trustee Relationships." Paper presented at the Association of Community College Trustees Southern/Northeast Region Seminar, Greensboro, N.C., June 6–8, 1996. (ED 395 644)

As representatives of their college and in working with the college community, community college trustees enter into numerous relationships, each of which has associated roles and responsibilities. Responsibilities of the board chair, for example, include working with the president to set meeting agenda, appointing committee members, serving as the official spokesperson for the board, overseeing other trustees, providing counsel for the president, and initiating periodic board evaluations. In addition, trustees in many colleges employ or appoint the college president, and it is important that a friendly trustee-president relationship exist. With respect to trustees' relationships with college administrative staff and faculty, the fundamental responsibility of the board is to provide them with adequate policies, rules, and regulations for effective operation of the institution. Faculty and staff, for their part, are directly responsible to the president and should conduct their business with the board through the president. The role of state governing boards varies; in North Carolina, the state board has full authority to adopt all policies, regulations, and standards deemed necessary for the operation of the system but traditionally grants maximum autonomy to the colleges. In that state, individual trustees have limited direct communication with state-level administrators but are the most powerful group of lobbyists, advocates, and public relations professionals that community colleges have in working with the state assembly and the U.S. Congress.

Fisher, J. L. *The Board and the President.* New York: Macmillan, 1991. 163 pp. (ED 328 207)

The author discusses the traditional roles of president and trustees and reviews research on leadership that suggests that policies and practices of most governing boards may be antithetical to effective presidential leadership. Approaches to the presidential search are analyzed, as well as potential stumbling blocks in the process of choosing a president. Models for evaluating the effectiveness of the president and the board are offered. The book concludes with a discussion of leadership responsibility, authority, and accountability. Appendixes include examples of institutional reviews, meeting agendas, compensation studies, and other relevant documents. Also includes 117 references.

Shared Governance Issues

Bryant, D. W. "New Leadership Considerations for Old Realities." *Community Junior College Quarterly of Research and Practice,* 1992, *16*(1), 77–84.

This article suggests ways to improve community college campus leadership delegation by understanding the faculty's historic role in academic areas, encouraging enhanced faculty participation in college governance, keeping channels of communication between faculty and board open, working jointly on affirmative action processes, maintaining a focus on leadership development, and identifying model institutions and mentors.

Nussbaum, T. J. *Evolving Community College Shared Governance to Better Serve the Public Interest.* Sacramento: California Community Colleges, 1995. 69 pp. (ED 397 922)

Intended to stimulate improvements in shared governance in the California community colleges, this report outlines the evolution and current structures of shared governance at the local and system levels and provides recommendations for change. The current, more formalized structure for institutional participation in systemwide policy making is seen as open and effective but vulnerable to weaknesses born of increased competition among institutions. The author provides recommendations for improving shared governance, including instituting a code of ethics, implementing multi-institutional councils, and giving districts the authority to create additional revenue. The proposed code of ethics is appended.

Franklin, J. D., and others. "Faculty Leadership: A Dynamic, Potent Force for Comprehensive Institutional Development." Paper presented at "Leadership 2000," the third annual conference on leadership development of the League for Innovation in the Community College, Chicago, Jul. 7–10, 1991. (ED 344 629)

Scholars and practitioners alike have called for a new style of leadership on community college campuses, where administrators and trustees should be capable of adapting and responding easily to an uncertain political and social climate. Although community colleges are rooted historically in a hierarchical leadership mode, there seems to be broad consensus today that collective leadership is more effective. In specific cases, faculty at community colleges have identified hierarchical leadership structures at their institutions as ineffectual and in need of change. However, despite the fact that community college faculty are uniquely qualified for, and desire, leadership roles in a collective model, divisions between the faculty and the administration restrict their leadership potential. Initiating a participatory leadership model requires new approaches and involves various steps: (1) building trust in a collective model, and among the various constituencies represented in such a model; (2) developing methods for information sharing among faculty, administrators, and boards of trustees; (3) forging dynamic interactions between the two coexisting paths for decision making (that is, administrative and academic), enabling primary members of each to cross-participate; (4) preserving faculty development in the face of budget problems by providing resources to enhance professional growth; (5) utilizing technology to help faculty and administrators engage in collective leadership efforts; and (6) instituting concrete systems of recognition and reward for faculty involvement. Includes seventeen references.

Future Challenges for Community College Leaders

Harris, Z. M., and others. "Leadership." *Community College Journal,* 1996, 66(5), 10–17.

As part of a theme issue (April–May 1996) entitled "Beyond the Mirror: Reflecting on Who We Are and Where We Need to Be," this article includes five essays by community college presidents and researchers discussing college leadership and the direction leaders must take in the future. Each president examines issues involving implementation of college programs, complexities of educational finance, utilization of part-time faculty, accountability, the effects of gender differences on leadership styles, leadership competencies, and the challenges and rewards of leadership positions.

Wallin, D. L., and Ryan, J. R. "Order out of Chaos: Leadership for the 21st Century." *Community College Journal of Research and Practice,* 1994, *18*(6), 527–538.

This article explores the effects of the current changes experienced by community colleges and the role that leaders must play to govern effectively. The authors suggest that successful leaders should have a well-articulated vision, anticipate change, act to empower the campus community, and acknowledge the right of individuals to fail. Contains fifteen references.

Schober, D. J., and Rosenthal, L. "Quality and Board Leadership." Paper presented at the annual Association of Community College Trustees Pacific Region Seminar, La Jolla, Calif., May 13–15, 1994. 37 pp. (ED 371 782) [For the annual report of the Commission on Quantum Quality, see ED 356 001.]

In February 1992, the Commission on Quantum Quality recommended that the Maricopa County Community College District (MCCCD) in Arizona launch a quality initiative that involved implementation of continuous quality improvement (CQI) and, based on John Carver's philosophy and model, active involvement of the MCCCD's board. Key principles behind the initiative included a customer focus, dedication to continuous improvement, a systematic approach to processes and their improvement, teamwork, and use of statistical methods for decision making. Influenced by Carver's ideas that board members should be active leaders, the MCCCD governing board became more involved in the development of the district's vision and mission and began to apply CQI to board meetings.

Association of Community College Trustees. *Trustee Quarterly.* (1993, four issues). Washington, D.C.: Association of Community College Trustees. 82 pp. (ED 367 412)

The four issues of *Trustee Quarterly* contained in this document focus on topics of concern to community college trustees. Included are articles on the prospects for educational reform during the first Clinton administration, strategies for obtaining needed resources from state legislatures, and the relationship between college chief executive officers and boards of trustees. The importance of trustee commitment to winning passage of community college bond referenda, as well as the role of community colleges in the global economy, is stressed, citing the experiences of Southwestern College in Chula Vista, California, with the North American Free Trade Agreement. The relationship between community colleges and the federal government is also discussed in articles on the role of trustees in federal advocacy.

Vaughan, G. B., and others. *Dilemmas of Leadership: Decision Making and Ethics in the Community College.* San Francisco: Jossey-Bass, 1992. [This document not available from EDRS. Contact publisher directly; $28.95. Outside U.S.: Maxwell Macmillan International Publishing Group, 866 Third Avenue, New York, NY 10022.]

Focusing primarily on issues that can be directly influenced by actions of the governing board or president, the nine chapters of this book explore the ethical dilemmas of leadership in today's community colleges. 1. "Leaders on a Tightrope: The Risks and Tensions of Community College Leadership," by G. B. Vaughan, provides an overview of some of the ethical dilemmas leaders face in education. 2. "The Fear of Knowing and the Ethics of Ignoring," by A. M. Cohen, examines a guiding ethos of community colleges and the ways in which data are collected and employed. 3. "The President as Moral Leader," by D. F. Moriarty, places the responsibility for ethical practices directly with the president. 4. "Ethics in Instructional Programs," by F. B. Brawer, looks at the need for community colleges to clearly enunciate criteria for ethical behavior. 5. "Academic Scruples: Faculty and Personnel Issues," by J. N. Hankin, offers examples of ethical dilemmas in student services, curricula, instructional activities, governance and college/community relations, budget and finance, and personnel matters. 6. "Business and Community Linkages," by K. A. Bowyer, examines the positive and negative results of these partnerships, pointing out pitfalls to avoid. 7. "Trustees and Governing Boards," by G. W. Davis, focuses on the role of these entities in setting an institution's ethical tone. 8. "Selecting and Developing Community College Leaders," by C. B. Neff, evaluates the ethical commitments inherent in the presidential search process. 9. "The Importance of Ethics in Good Administrative Practice," by J. B. Tatum, sums up points made in the previous chapters and criticizes trustees and presidents for skirting ethical issues.

Additional References

Bensimon, E. M. "Understanding Administrative Work." In A. Cohen, F. Brawer, and Associates (eds.), *Managing Community Colleges: A Handbook for Effective Practice.* San Francisco: Jossey-Bass, 1994.

Higher Education Research Institute. *A Social Change Model of Leadership Development.* Los Angeles: University of California, Los Angeles, 1996.

Wren, J. T. *The Leader's Companion: Insights on Leadership Through the Ages.* New York: The Free Press, 1995.

LUCY LEE is publications coordinator for the ERIC Clearinghouse for Community Colleges.

INDEX

ORDERING INFORMATION

NEW DIRECTIONS FOR COMMUNITY COLLEGES is a series of paperback books that provides expert assistance to help community colleges meet the challenges of their distinctive and expanding educational mission. Books in the series are published quarterly in Spring, Summer, Fall, and Winter and are available for purchase by subscription and individually.

SUBSCRIPTIONS cost $55.00 for individuals (a savings of 37 percent over single-copy prices) and $98.00 for institutions, agencies, and libraries. Please do not send institutional checks for personal subscriptions. Standing orders are accepted. Prices subject to change. (For subscriptions outside of North America, add $7.00 for shipping via surface mail or $25.00 for air mail. Orders *must be prepaid* in U.S. dollars by check drawn on a U.S. bank or charged to VISA, MasterCard, or American Express.)

SINGLE COPIES cost $22.00 plus shipping (see below) when payment accompanies order. California, New Jersey, New York, and Washington, D.C., residents please include appropriate sales tax. Canadian residents add GST and any local taxes. Billed orders will be charged shipping and handling. No billed shipments to post office boxes. (Orders from outside North America *must be prepaid* in U.S. dollars by check drawn on a U.S. bank or charged to VISA, MasterCard, or American Express.)

SHIPPING (SINGLE COPIES ONLY): $30.00 and under, add 5.50; to $50.00 add $6.50; to $75.00, add $7.50; to $100.00, add $9.00; to $150.00, add $10.00.

DISCOUNTS FOR QUANTITY ORDERS are available. Please write to the address below for information.

ALL ORDERS must include either the name of an individual or an official purchase order number. Please submit your order as follows:
  Subscriptions: specify series and year subscription is to begin
  Single copies: include individual title code (such as CC82)

MAIL ALL ORDERS TO:
  Jossey-Bass Publishers
  350 Sansome Street
  San Francisco, California 94104-1342

FOR SUBSCRIPTION SALES OUTSIDE OF THE UNITED STATES, contact any international subscription agency or Jossey-Bass directly.

OTHER TITLES AVAILABLE IN THE
NEW DIRECTIONS FOR COMMUNITY COLLEGES SERIES
Arthur M. Cohen, Editor-in-Chief
Florence B. Brawer, Associate Editor